SHAKESPEARE'S GARDENS

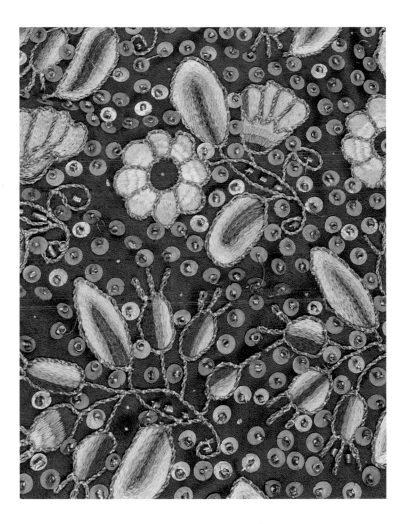

SHAKESPEARE'S GARDENS

Jackie Bennett

Photographs by Andrew Lawson

FRANCES LINCOLN

In association with the

NOTE ON THE PLAYS

For consistency this book uses the dates accepted by the Shakespeare Birthplace Trust for the composition of Shakespeare's works (see page 188). Quotations taken from the plays are from Stanley Wells, Gary Taylor, John Jowett and William Montgomery (eds) (2005), *The Oxford Shakespeare: The Complete Works.* Oxford: Clarendon Press.

Frances Lincoln Limited
74–77 White Lion Street
London N1 9PF

Shakespeare's Gardens
Copyright © Frances Lincoln Limited 2016
Text © Jackie Bennett 2016
Photographs copyright © see page 192
First Frances Lincoln edition 2016

A catalogue record for this book is available from the British Library.

ISBN 978-0-7112-3726-1

Designed by Anne Wilson

Printed and bound in China

1 2 3 4 5 6 7 8 9

Quarto is the authority on a wide range of topics.

Quarto educates, entertains and enriches the lives of our readers – enthusiasts and lovers of hands-on living.

www.QuartoKnows.com

HALF-TITLE The Elizabethans carried sweet-smelling herbs and dried flowers in embroidered bags, like this one in silk and satin with metal thread.
TITLE PAGES The gardens at Mary Arden's Farm in Wilmcote include the birthplace of Shakespeare's mother (page 2) and Palmer's Farm (page 3).
RIGHT Foxgloves (*Digitalis purpurea*) growing at Mary Arden's Farm.

Contents

Introduction

$\mathcal{B}$ OOKS ABOUT SHAKESPEARE often begin by saying that we know little about his life – and in one sense that is true. We have an outline of dates: he was baptized at Holy Trinity Church, Stratford-upon-Avon on 26 April 1564; married in November 1582; and was buried on 23 April 1616 on, or just before, his fifty-second birthday. The few documents that bear his name tell us that he was working in London from his mid-twenties, returning to Stratford intermittently, and probably for much longer periods in his last decade. Yet this biographical apology ignores one very large body of visible evidence for the life and times of William Shakespeare – the houses and gardens in which he and his family lived.

In association with the Shakespeare Birthplace Trust (SBT),[1] which cares for the family homes and which holds a wealth of visual and written material about the playwright, this book brings together what we know about his own gardens and those that he could have known and visited – in London, Warwickshire and elsewhere. It is both a celebration of his life and an investigation into a central aspect of Shakespeare's world.

A TRAVELLING MAN

Every writer has to make their own Shakespeare 'journey'. Mine started in early 2015, on a muddy lane in a village just south of Stratford-upon-Avon, where I was about to take up a writers' residency and begin work on this book.[2] The lane is part of a south–north footpath called Shakespeare's Way, which leads from the Globe Theatre on the south bank of the River Thames, in London, to Henley Street in the market town of Stratford-upon-Avon. It is an approximation of the 160-kilometre/100-mile or more journey William Shakespeare would have taken, through Oxford and the Chilterns, to and from his home town. On foot, the journey can take a week to ten days. On horseback, along roads rutted by the carters taking goods to and from the capital city, it took three to four days each way. How often Shakespeare would have made this journey no one knows, but commuting was regular from Stratford-upon-Avon to London, especially when the professional theatres were closed in Lent and during times of plague outbreaks.

In the Warwickshire village of Clifford Chambers, a lane lined with lime (*Tilia*) trees is traversed by Shakespeare's Way – a long-distance footpath from London to Stratford-upon-Avon.

Shakespeare lived in an age when exploration and map making were at the fore. The first county maps of Britain included Saxton's 1576 map of Shakespeare's county, Warwickshire, and the adjoining one of Leicestershire.

Shakespeare was born into an age of travel and adventure. Queen Elizabeth I was on the throne, and when William was sixteen years old Francis Drake returned to England from his three-year circumnavigation of the globe. The first maps of Britain and the world were in circulation and, in 1588, the Spanish Armada dropped anchor in the English Channel. In 1594, Walter Raleigh sailed off to South America to find the fabled 'city of gold' – El Dorado. Shakespeare would live to see the Gunpowder Plot of 1605 and the first permanent English settlement in Virginia, in 1607.

In terms of gardening, it was also exciting times, as plants were arriving from the Old and the New Worlds: nasturtiums (*Tropaeolum majus*) from Peru; marigolds (*Tagetes*) from Mexico; and hibiscus from Asia. According to topographer William Harrison in his *Historicall Description of the Island of Britain* in 1587, gardens had improved immeasurably in the previous four decades – no doubt because of these new plants.[3] Although the religious break with Rome in the 1530s meant that cultural contact with Italy was restricted, the classical ideas of the Italian Renaissance gardens did filter into Britain, particularly in the early seventeenth century. Meanwhile, fashionable gardeners looked towards France and the Low Countries for their inspiration.

Shakespeare's work reflects this growing interest in imported plants, herbs, spices and other foods to which he was exposed in London. Yet, while he had one foot in this new, outward-looking world, he had the other firmly planted in Stratford-upon-Avon – a traditional market town. When he came home after a six-month absence he would enter the town over Clopton Bridge – just as visitors do today. Sometimes, there would be changes – fires destroyed parts of Stratford-upon-Avon in the 1590s and plague would certainly have taken the lives of friends that he knew – but essentially he was coming home from the city to a country town, a place that would nurture his lifelong interest in flowers, plants and gardens.

GARDENS IN SHAKESPEARE'S WORK

O, what pity is it
That he had not so trimmed and dressed his land
As we this garden!
Richard II, Act 3 scene 4

In this scene the queen overhears her gardeners talking about the state of the nation under her husband's rule, comparing it to a neglected garden. The whole land is choked with weeds, the fruit trees left unpruned, the knots are in disarray and the plants swarming with caterpillars. In this short scene, Shakespeare gives us the gamut of gardening tasks – supporting the limbs of heavy-fruiting, espaliered apricots so as not to break the stems, deadheading too-tall plants and lopping branches off fruit trees. *Richard II* was written in 1595, a couple of years before Shakespeare bought his own house and garden at New Place but it certainly sounds like its author has been – or at least seen – a gardener at work.

Shakespeare himself was both a playwright and a working actor, not the star of his theatre company. *Richard II* is one of the many times that we hear working people speak in Shakespeare, and it is fitting that it is the gardeners who are gossiping. They are knowledgeable and informed about current affairs; they are people who care about their country and what is happening to it and have pride in their work. Gardeners are often nameless in the records of those making gardens, yet Shakespeare gives them their moment of glory.

'There is no ancient gentlemen but gardeners'
Hamlet, Act 5 scene 1

'Get ye all three into the box-tree'

Twelfth Night, Act 2 scene 5

This twentieth-century interpretation of a knot garden was designed by the great plantswoman Rosemary Verey, at her home, Barnsley House, in Gloucestershire, UK.

All the elements of the ordered universe that made up a typical Elizabethan garden can be found in Shakespeare's plays: *allées* and walks, mazes and knots, galleries and viewing platforms, orchards, parks and arbours. Three characters in *Twelfth Night* hide from Malvolio in a box (*Buxus*) tree; in *Love's Labour's Lost*, a tryst takes place close to the 'curious-knotted garden';[4] and, in *Henry IV Part II*, Falstaff is encouraged to stay a while in Judge Shallow's orchard.[5] Parks and gardens are used for playing bowls, for hunting, for eating and, most importantly, for deceptions, misunderstandings and dramatic unravellings. Many of the settings of Shakespeare's plays have an 'otherworldly' quality about them, but placing the action in a garden, a wood or a park makes them down to earth and familiar.

GARDENS AS THEATRE

If there can be any doubt that gardens were the height of theatrical interest in Shakespeare's lifetime, we only need to refer to the *Maske of Flowers*, which was performed by the Gentlemen of Gray's Inn, at Whitehall before the king and queen on Twelfth Night 1614, to celebrate the recent marriage of the Earl of Somerset to Frances Howard, daughter of the Earl of Suffolk.

A booklet printed in 1614 to celebrate the event tells of a huge stage production that would rival the great gardens of Kenilworth, Theobalds and Richmond Palace. It demonstrated that stage sets could be very elaborate, and it also cements the idea of gardens as a setting for theatre – and theatres as a setting for gardens.

The Whitehall performance involved a stage set of a garden: 'The curtains being drawn was seen a Garden of strange beauty, cast into four-quarters with a cross-walk and alleys compassing each Quarter.'[6] The garden was on an impressive scale, surrounded by a brick wall, with a fountain held up by silver columns holding a bowl 2.75 metre/9 feet off the ground and 7.5 metres/25 feet across. Above, stood a 1 metre/3 feet-high golden Neptune, holding a trident.

The quarters of the garden were contained by low hedges of 'cypress and juniper and the knots within were set with artificial flowers'. There were pots of gillyflowers (*Dianthus caryophyllus*), tulips and even a garden mount with an arbour of artificial eglantine roses (*Rosa rubiginosa*) and honeysuckle (*Lonicera*). The arbour alone was 10 metres/33 feet long and 6.4 metres/21 feet high, divided into six arches.

Throughout Shakespeare's lifetime, gardens evolved from necessary food-producing plots to fashionable, flower-filled showpieces. Shakespeare lived through those stages: as a boy on his mother's farm; as a young man in London where he probably visited more gardens than at any other time in his life; and as a mature man in Stratford where he created his own garden.

A LITERARY FLOWERING

The flowers referred to in Shakespeare's plays and poems have been – particularly in the Victorian period – the main focus of any book purporting to be about Shakespeare's gardens. Authors such as Sidney Beisley, the Reverend Henry Ellacombe and J. Harvey Bloom revived interest in the wild and cultivated flowers used in his work. Shakespeare had an intuitive knowledge of wild flowers as well as a growing interest in the new plants that were arriving in the late sixteenth and early seventeenth century. Alongside his literary sources of Holinshed, Horace and Ovid, Shakespeare must have had a reference copy of John Gerard's *Herball* of 1597 (see panel, page 130).

Anyone who has watched or read a Shakespeare play or sonnet will know that the natural world was part and parcel of his thought and speech. His upbringing in the town garden and orchard of his birthplace, on his mother's farm and in the fields of Shottery and Wilmcote goes some way to explain how flowers and plants became such an effortless part of his language. In *Cymbeline*, Shakespeare describes the inside of a cowslip (*Primula veris*) as if he had lain down and peered inside, and he pays similar close scrutiny to daffodils and marigolds in *The Winter's Tale*. He can accurately name the cornfield weeds in King Lear's 'crown' – fumitory, burdocks, nettles, darnel and thistles – as only one who has first-hand knowledge of them could do. Shakespeare came from farming stock and his father's and his mother's heritage was the cultivation of the Warwickshire countryside.

A PICTURE OF SHAKESPEARE

Until recently there were just two images that could be directly linked to Shakespeare with no dispute – but both were created after his death.[7] Most familiar is the engraving by Martin Droeshout the Younger created for the frontispiece of the book now known as the First Folio, the printed collection of plays produced and printed by Shakespeare's friends in 1623. The other likeness is a bust in his parish church of Holy Trinity in Stratford-upon-Avon – both depict Shakespeare in later life.

In 2006, the National Portrait Gallery made their 'Chandos' portrait – thought to be by John Taylor and dating to the first decade of the seventeenth century – the centre of an exhibition entitled *Searching for Shakespeare*. Since then, a new painting has come to light, known as the Cobbe portrait. This shows a younger, more vivid and well-dressed man. It belonged to the family of the third Earl of Southampton, Henry Wriothesley – the man to whom he dedicated his first full-length works, *Venus and Adonis* and *The Rape of Lucrece*, written in 1592–3 and 1593–4 respectively. Although the artist is unknown, the painting is thought to be the source for many of the later Shakespeare images.

BELOW Probably the most famous image of the playwright is the engraving by Droeshout, printed in 1623 in *Mr William Shakespeares Comedies, Histories, & Tragedies*, better known as the First Folio.

OPPOSITE The Cobbe portrait of William Shakespeare (named after the family who own it) was painted from life *c.*1610. It is most likely to have been commissioned and owned by Henry Wriothesley, the third Earl of Southampton.

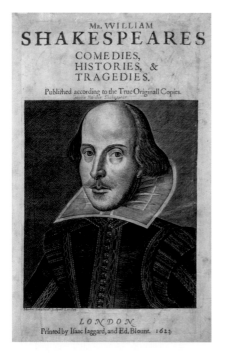

> 'Keep these flowers.
> We'll see how close art
> can come near their
> colours'
>
> *The Two Noble Kinsmen,*
> Act 2 scene 2

There are several copies of the Cobbe portrait in existence, painted within a few years of the original – another clue that the sitter was famous enough for people to want to have their own one. One of these early copies now hangs in the exhibition space of the Shakespeare Centre, right next to the house where Shakespeare was born, in Henley Street, Stratford-upon-Avon.

Each of the family homes has a place in Shakespeare's story, beginning with his birthplace in Henley Street. Next is his mother's family home, Mary Arden's Farm, in the nearby village of Wilmcote; it comprises 28 hectares/70 acres of food-producing gardens, pastures and meadows. Representing the youthful Shakespeare is the quintessential English country garden, Anne Hathaway's Cottage in Shottery, which has been the subject of more paintings than any other domestic Tudor house. There is his daughter Susanna's house and garden, Hall's Croft, built a few years after her marriage to the doctor, John Hall. Finally, there is Shakespeare's own house – or rather his garden – New Place, now a Grade II listed park and garden that continues to intrigue us with its archaeology and to offer more clues to his life in the town.

Four centuries is a long time in the life of a garden. Shakespeare's gardens today have elements of Tudor and Jacobean design and planting within them, but they are not recreations of sixteenth- or early seventeenth-century gardens. To those used to visiting gardens this will not seem strange. Very few gardens are recreated totally in the period of the house, but tend to illustrate a succession of periods and styles. In the case of the Stratford gardens, they each have a complex and multilayered history which is part of their character. Rather than wiping this out in favour of historical recreation, the SBT has allowed each of the five gardens to present their own 'faces' – be they Tudor, High Victorian, Edwardian or mid-twentieth century.

In this book, I hope to use the gardens as a way to piece together another aspect of Shakespeare's life. What were the gardens like when he lived in Stratford – how have they changed and developed – and what was the cultural context in which he was writing and gardening? This exploration will take us from the palaces of Whitehall to the simplest rural Warwickshire dwelling, and will show that Shakespeare was a man who, in gardens as in his work, spanned all these worlds.

Simple country flowers and herbs grow in the gardens at Mary Arden's Farm, where Shakespeare's mother grew up.

Shakespeare's World
Tudor Gardens

And bid her steal into the pleached bower
Where honeysuckles, ripened by the sun,
Forbid the sun to enter

Much Ado About Nothing, Act 3 scene 1

Shakespeare was born into an age in which gardens were an integral part of cultural life at every level of society. From the royal palaces of London to the town and country houses of the gentry, garden style was beginning to filter from the top down. Henry VIII set the trend for lavish spending on parks and gardens, and Elizabeth I's courtiers followed suit. In this chapter, we explore the gardens of Shakespeare's time and particularly those that he might have known. It was a world where flowers and plants were to be admired, not only outdoors but also indoors – on everything from dress to household decor.

Textiles decorated with stylized images of plants and flowers, as on this gentleman's nightcap held by the Shakespeare Birthplace Trust, were fashionable until the first quarter of the seventeenth century.

ELIZABETHAN GARDENS sit within the framework of the Tudor age that began after the Battle of Bosworth in 1485 – the event that marked the end of the Wars of the Roses. In *Henry VI Part I*, Shakespeare sets the memorable scene in which the nobles must choose their allegiance to York or Lancaster (by plucking a white or a red rose) in London's Temple Garden.[1] When, in *Richard III*, Shakespeare has the warring houses united with a rose he was well aware of its significance to his current queen, before whom his plays would be performed many times. Under Henry VIII and his children Edward, Mary and Elizabeth, the combined red and white Tudor rose became one of the most potent symbols of unity and strength.

Tudor gardens would go on to surpass medieval gardens in many ways, not least in the amount of money lavished on them. According to historian Christopher Thacker: 'Garden history in Britain begins as a full, coherent and unified subject in the reign of Queen Elizabeth I.'[2] Henry VIII had put gardens at the heart of his palace-building programme and started a trend which his daughter followed – that of exuberance, display and bold colours. Elizabeth, who was more careful with the royal purse, did not build any new gardens, but her subjects would compete to impress her with the lavish embellishment of their own grounds.

WHAT DID AN ELIZABETHAN GARDEN LOOK LIKE?

Although there are few surviving intact Elizabethan gardens, we actually know a lot about them. From archaeology, documentary records, paintings and literature we can draw up an impressive list of gardens of the higher ranks of society and have a good idea of what they looked like. One of the reasons there is so little left for us to see on the ground is that gardens were, in a large part, ephemeral – created for show and made of natural materials, timber, small shrubs, climbers and short-lived perennials.

They have naturally decayed or been swept away as fashions changed, yet their style is unmistakable. In terms of layout, neatness was highly prized, so Elizabethan gardens often had geometric layouts with rectangular beds. Garden plots were surrounded with pales (wooden fencing) usually of oak but sometimes other woods painted in bright colours. The planting within the beds would encompass a wide range of flowers and fruits, both native and increasingly imported species, as well as herbs for household and medicinal use. There would invariably be a plant-covered arbour ('herber') and a covered timber walk (*allée*), with climbing plants to give shade.

If space allowed, the typical Elizabethan property would have a square or rectangular open space, known as a 'court', leading on to fruit trees and orchards, and sometimes a knot garden. Art historian Sir Roy Strong gives

'We will unite the white rose and the red'
Richard III, Act 5 scene 8

In *Henry VI Part I*, the nobles must choose a white or a red rose to show their allegiance to either York or the Crown. Shakespeare sets this scene in London's Temple Garden.

Roses

Of all flowers
Methinks a rose is best
The Two Noble Kinsmen, Act 2 scene 2

What's in a name? That which we call a rose
By any other word would smell as sweet
Romeo and Juliet, Act 2 scene 1

Long before Shakespeare's time the political power of the Houses of York and Lancaster had been set – not in stone – but in flowers. The red rose of Lancaster (*Rosa gallica* var. *officinalis*) and the white rose of York (*R. × alba*) were united when Henry VII married Elizabeth of York and he created a new royal emblem – the Tudor rose. With its red outer and white inner petals, it became a potent symbol of the dynasty, fashioned in carved wood, leather *mâché* and stone on to ceilings and panelling, and worked into tapestries, embroidered textiles and dress fabric. The Tudor rose remained the royal symbol throughout the reigns of Henry VIII, his son Edward and his daughters Mary and Elizabeth.

Shakespeare was well aware of the meaning of the symbolism of the rose when researching for his two sequences of history plays. The Temple Garden scene in *Henry VI Part I*, Act 2 scene 4 has the most references to roses of any Shakespeare play.

WILD BRIARS

The roses that Shakespeare grew up with are those of the English field and hedgerow: eglantine rose or sweet briar (*R. rubiginosa*), with its leaves that smell of apple when they are crushed; burnet rose (*R. spinosissima*), with its black hips; and dog rose (*R. canina*). Perhaps coincidentally, the Temple Garden in London was for the use of the legal profession and the colloquial name for dog rose in Warwickshire was 'lawyers'. Eglantine rose was also the rose most often used to symbolize Queen Elizabeth I and became her personal flower motif.

It is these wild roses that Shakespeare writes about most often, although he often combines them with those he would have seen in gardens – musk roses (*R. moschata*) and damask roses (*R. × damascena*) – which had been grown from the eleventh century onwards. The bank in *A Midsummer Night's Dream* is 'quite overcanopied with . . . sweet musk-roses and with eglantine'.[3] John Gerard is quite dismissive of the wild kinds, saying that the 'brier bush' (dog rose) is not worthy of a place in his garden. Interestingly, Gerard notes that a 'double white rose' grows wild in Lancashire – probably *R. × alba* 'Alba Semiplena'.

PRACTICAL USES

Roses were not only important symbolically in Shakespeare's world but also practically. They were used for cooking, preserving, perfume and cosmetics as well as medical remedies. Shakespeare's son-in-law, Dr John Hall, listed sixty uses of the plant in his medical case notes (see page 139). The petals were introduced to flavour junkets, jellies, cakes and sauces, or distilled into rose water; medicinal powders were made from the seeds; essences and oils were extracted from the petals and leaves; and the hips were cooked in tarts and pies. Roses were indispensable and, although rose petals could be bought from markets and apothecaries (*R. gallica* var. *officinalis* is known as the apothecary's rose), they were already widely grown as garden plants.

OPPOSITE, CLOCKWISE FROM TOP LEFT Damask rose (*Rosa × damascena*) from John Gerard's *Herball*; apothecary's rose (*R. gallica* var. *officinalis*); eglantine rose (*R. rubiginosa*); and dog rose (*R. canina*)

The Tudor garden at Penshurst Place in Kent features brightly painted posts with heraldic figures, which were typical of the period.

an imaginative evocation of what it was like to walk in a Tudor garden: 'The walls are covered with espaliered pear, apple and damson trees, the roses of York and Lancaster scent the air and everywhere . . . there will be a forest of pinnacles bearing brightly coloured heraldic beasts, their gilding catching the sunlight.'[4] The Elizabethan period is, according to Strong, when the Pleasure Garden becomes the essential component of the Great House.[5]

PATTERNS WOVEN IN SILKEN THREAD

The Elizabethans loved pattern and design, which can be seen on everything from gowns to bedcoverings. Textiles were hung from bedposts, carpets (too precious to walk on) were used to cover tables and, if an Elizabethan wanted to show off their status, it would be with embroidered wall hangings and Flemish curtains known as an 'arras', stitched in wool or silk on linen. Arras became a general term for stage curtains and is used frequently in Shakespeare as somewhere for characters to hide while listening in on conversations. Many of these textiles were imported from the continent and depicted stylized floral patterns, which translated easily into gardens. Embroidery patterns, which could be found in pattern books, were soon plundered for gardens – and vice versa. The black silk stitching known as blackwork was particularly suitable for depicting knots and mazes.[6]

LEFT This typical enclosed garden with rectangular plots and trellis fencing, all enclosed by wooden pales, appeared in *The Gardeners Labyrinth* by Thomas Hill, in 1577.

BELOW Little Moreton Hall in Shropshire is one of the most individual Tudor houses in the UK and was built in stages throughout the sixteenth century. The knot garden follows a later pattern, of 1670.

BELOW LEFT AND BELOW RIGHT
Tudor gardeners were encouraged to
install more and more elaborate knots,
as shown in Thomas Hill's *Gardeners
Labyrinth* (1577). The patterns echoed
those already used for embroidery.
OPPOSITE ABOVE An embroidered
silk pillow from the early 1600s
depicts flowers that were fashionable
at the time, including roses, tulips,
irises and snake's-head fritillaries
(*Fritillaria meleagris*).
OPPOSITE BELOW LEFT AND BELOW
RIGHT Gervase Markham described
two types of knot garden: an 'open'
knot (left) with no infill; and a 'closed'
knot (right) which is planted with
flowers of a single type.

In Shakespeare's lifetime, patterns for simple knot gardens would have been taken from Thomas Hill's 1577 book *The Gardeners Labyrinth* or from French books such as Estienne and Liébault's *Maison Rustique* (1600).[7] What we think of today as a knot garden – a decorative shape laid out in box (*Buxus*) hedging – was not typical of the period. Elizabethan knots used aromatic shrubs such as lavender and santolina or herbs such as hyssop, germander (*Teucrium*) and savory (*Satureja*) to give shape in winter. Sometimes, it was the beds themselves that formed the 'knot' or pattern. So that the design could be seen more easily – particularly from important rooms overlooking the gardens – the ground surface would be made of different-coloured sands, crushed brick and stone to set off the pattern. Gervase Markham, writing in 1613, spelt out the difference between 'open' and 'closed' knots: open being those with no infill other than the ground surface; closed being those filled with flowers of a single colour such as gillyflowers and sweet Williams (*Dianthus*), primroses and violets.[8]

Box (*Buxus*) as a garden plant became more fashionable and more widely used in the early seventeenth century. The famous apothecary and herbalist John Parkinson, writing in 1629, recommends it, saying 'it serveth very well to set out a knot or border or any beds, for besides that it is ever-greene, it be reasonable thick set, will easily be cut and formed into any fashion . . .'

Queen Elizabeth I travelled frequently between her palaces and the houses of her courtiers.

THE ROYAL PALACES

Fashion in gardening, as in clothes, jewellery and even shoes, trickled downwards through the various strata of Tudor society, but it was royalty who were setting the trend, commissioning the most cutting-edge designs for their gardens. Elizabeth I had many palaces in regular use including Windsor, Richmond, Nonsuch, Whitehall, Hampton Court and Greenwich along the River Thames. The queen was born at Greenwich and died at Richmond, and spent a lot of time at the waterside palaces and their gardens, each of which had a landing stage on the river. Along with the Lord Chamberlain's Men acting company, Shakespeare performed many times at court. The queen did not go to the theatre – the theatre came to the queen.

WHITEHALL

Whitehall was the epicentre of Elizabeth I's power. It occupied at least 9 hectares/22 acres of ground beside the river in the centre of London. It began life as Cardinal Wolsey's York Place, until his removal by Henry VIII, who immediately started work to remodel it as a palace ready to receive his queen, Anne Boleyn, in 1533. It had 1,500 rooms including a great hall, chapel, long gallery and great chamber – all destroyed by fire in 1698. Outside, Henry created a rectangular garden bounded by brick walls, with raised brick flower beds, topped with white- and green-painted railings, a big, three-storey fountain (fountains were not commonplace in Tudor gardens). It had an open loggia along one wall, and an elaborate sundial. In 1584, a visitor called Leopold van Wedel recorded that he had counted thirty-four gilded heraldic beasts set on painted poles around the garden. This garden is the first real garden to be depicted in a British painting – *The Family of Henry VIII* by an unknown artist.

Whitehall also had an orchard, covered tennis courts and areas for playing bowls, practising archery and jousting. It was bounded on one side by the River Thames and on the other by an extensive park. Today, Horse Guards Parade in London overlays a small part of this vast palace.

Shakespeare's life as a playwright and actor was intricately entwined with the ebb and flow of state power. On St Stephen's Day[9] 1606, shortly after the Gunpowder Plot which had almost killed King James I and his entourage, Shakespeare and his company performed *King Lear* to the court at Whitehall.[10] Whether or not he spent time in the gardens, he would have been familiar with the layout of this vast palace and of the other out-of-town royal residences, including Hampton Court.

The painting known as *The Family of Henry VIII* includes a glimpse of the gardens at Whitehall, through the arched openings.

HAMPTON COURT

Shakespeare would also have performed at Hampton Court with the Lord Chamberlain's Men and later with the King's Men. King James was there for his first Christmas festivities in 1603–4 when the King's Men performed in front of the court.

Hampton Court was largely the creation of Elizabeth I's father, Henry VIII, who fashioned a new house around a medieval core. Henry was often trying to emulate or surpass what was going on in France, particularly at Francis I's Fontainebleau, and he spent £62,000 on the extensions and gardens to show his wealth, power and prosperity. Here he introduced heraldic posts painted in white and green (the Tudor colours) topped with carved arms, the Tudor rose, mythical beasts such as dragons, and real beasts such as lions to symbolize strength.

There were also numerous sundials and clocks; timekeeping was a growing interest throughout the Tudor period. The gardens were compartmentalized into: a walled Privy Garden, designed to be viewed from the royal apartments, which offered a place of privacy and security away from the rest of the palace; a Mount Garden with a snail mount (so-called because of the winding paths on its slopes, to enable people to reach the top, resembled the shell of a snail); and kitchen gardens, which have recently been recreated for twenty-first century visitors. At the top of the mount was a dazzling, three-storey, glass arbour with an onion-shaped dome – designed to overlook the other gardens.

BELOW LEFT Henry VIII's interest in timekeeping is displayed by the Astronomical Clock he had put up at Hampton Court between 1540 and 1542.
BELOW RIGHT Hampton Court Palace on the River Thames lies downstream from Windsor.
OPPOSITE The sunken gardens at Hampton Court were once fish ponds for the royal household.

THE 'LOST' PALACES: RICHMOND, GREENWICH AND NONSUCH

Several of Elizabeth's palaces no longer exist, but they are certainly places that Shakespeare would have known. In February 1599, the court was at Richmond and the Lord Chamberlain's Men gave a Shrovetide performance, for which Shakespeare wrote a special prologue for the queen, mentioning the sundial in the gardens.

Elizabeth I liked to stay at Richmond in cold weather, as it was the warmest of her palaces, and she retreated to 'that winter box to shelter my old age'.[11] It was known to have had a Great Court, and a Great Orchard, as well as enclosed gardens, surrounded by covered galleries where the court could walk and play games in wet weather. Elizabeth spent her final Christmas there in 1602, and Shakespeare's company gave their last performance to her at Richmond Palace on 2 February 1603.[12]

Greenwich is another of the 'lost' waterside Tudor palaces, and it consisted of three great courtyards and a substantial park. One of the earliest performances by the Lord Chamberlain's Men of *A Midsummer Night's Dream* was before the queen in early 1595, at Greenwich.

Most enigmatic of all is Nonsuch Palace in Surrey, built by Henry VIII between 1538 and 1547, probably because it stood in such good hunting country. It was sold to the earls of Arundel, and in the 1580s had an overhaul by Lord John Lumley, who welcomed Queen Elizabeth there on many occasions. Lumley was an eccentric who embellished the garden with every outdoor

Elizabeth I divided her time between her waterside palaces, including the old palace of Greenwich.

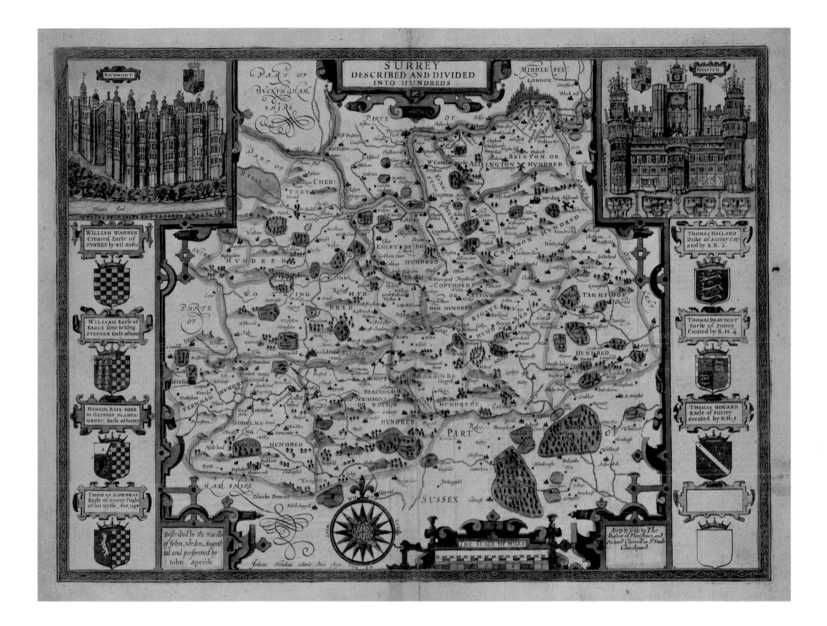

John Speed's map of Surrey, first published in 1611, includes illustrations of the now lost palaces of Richmond and Nonsuch.

entertainment including a banqueting house on a mound (a three-storey, brick building where residents would retire after dinner to take their dessert or drinks). The formal gardens had covered walks, *allées*, knots, fountains, marble basins and the beginnings of Italianate and Renaissance influences. Lumley was a Catholic and had more interest in Italian sculpture than his Protestant contemporaries, but he still adorned the garden with the usual allegorical references to the queen, including a fountain and a temple featuring Diana.

Nonsuch reverted to the crown in 1591, although Lumley continued to live there. Reports from visitor Thomas Platter reveal that it had some quirky

ABOVE In an effort to win Queen Elizabeth I's hand in marriage, Robert Dudley, the Earl of Leicester created extravagant gardens for her visit of 1575.

OPPOSITE The Privy Garden at Kenilworth Castle with its huge fountain is still approached through the old Norman keep, just as Elizabeth would have done.

animal topiary fashioned as if in chase: 'dogs, hares, all overgrown with plants, most artfully set out, so that from a distance one would take for real ones'.[13]

The topiary would be typical of an Elizabethan garden and would comprise evergreens such as ivy (*Hedera*) or rosemary trained to follow the outline of bent willow (*Salix*) twigs in the shape of figures and animals. Mazes were not high hedges, but 'foot' mazes, based on medieval contemplative ones. They would be cut to just 30–60 centimetres/1–2 feet in height and were also evergreen.

DUDLEY'S KENILWORTH

There was one house that tried to rival all the royal palaces of England in Elizabeth's reign and that was Kenilworth Castle, 25 kilometres/15½ miles from Shakespeare's home in Warwickshire. It is now the site of the most authentic recreation of an Elizabethan garden to date.

In July 1575, when Shakespeare was eleven years old, there would have been great excitement in Stratford-upon-Avon about the approaching visit of Queen Elizabeth to the home of Robert Dudley, Earl of Leicester, who had vastly rebuilt the castle in the hope of winning Elizabeth's hand in marriage. She was to stay for nineteen days, and the festivities planned were to be on a scale that had never been seen before. As a boy, Shakespeare could not have failed to hear about it – one of the imaginary scenes in *A Midsummer Night's Dream* is believed to have been inspired by the spectacle.

This was Dudley's last chance to impress – the queen had visited him several times previously, but remained unmoved by his advances. The park to the south-west of the castle was ornamented with seats and bowers, and the park as well as the mere – a huge artificial lake – became the backdrop for masques, dancing, fireworks, plays, dialogues and pageants. Elizabeth I approached Kenilworth over the top of a dam built to hold back the water and was greeted by the 'Lady of the Lake', adorned with flowers. Inside, Dudley had added a new lodgings building and a gatehouse to the already impressive medieval castle. He commissioned an actor, George Gascoigne, to write and design the festivities, which were, in essence, a series of set pieces of classical literature. Dudley was the patron of the Queen's Men – the official state theatre group – so perhaps they were the troupe that performed there that summer.

Dudley wanted to create a spectacle that no one would forget – a garden fit for a queen. Within the castle walls, 0.4 hectares/1 acre of ground was given over to a completely new Privy Garden, divided into quarters with paths of sand, edged with grass, and decorated with obelisks of purple 'porphyry' and a huge Carrera marble fountain topped with Dudley's heraldic device – a ragged staff. Fruit trees adorned the garden, as well as an aviary encrusted with jewels and filled with birds.

THE PRIVY GARDEN RECREATED

In 2009, English Heritage, the organization which cares for Kenilworth, decided to recreate the Privy Garden.[14] Normally, a Privy Garden would have been directly beneath the owner's or the important visitor's apartments for viewing, but at Kenilworth the only piece of level ground suitable for Dudley to build on was just inside the castle's north walls. Thus, the Privy Garden is approached through the old Norman keep, which emerges on to a raised viewing terrace – built specifically for Elizabeth I's visit.

There is a long and ebullient letter from a member of Dudley's household, Robert Langham. Langham tells us how Adrian, the gardener, helped him to creep into the Privy Garden while the queen was out hunting. He had clearly seen nothing like it in his life: 'a garden so appointed to feel the pleasant whisking wind above, or delectable coolness of the fountain-spring beneath to taste of delicious strawberries, cherries and other fruits . . . to smell such fragrancy of sweet odours, breathing from the plants, herbs and flowers . . .'[15]

Rosemary, sage (*Salvia*) and santolina, interspersed at intervals by standard and cones of clipped bay (*Laurus nobilis*) and hollies (*Ilex*), had been used for structure. In terms of flowers, Langham was silent, but in the Kenilworth scheme today the emphasis is on scent, using pinks (*Dianthus*), stocks (*Matthiola*), sweet Williams (*Dianthus barbatus*) and violets. Each quarter of the garden is subdivided into two knots, and the quarters are enclosed with low hedges of eglantine roses (*Rosa rubiginosa*) and hawthorn (*Crataegus*).

There is one more intellectual link between Kenilworth and the boy from Stratford-upon-Avon. The dominating marble fountain in the centre is carved with panels depicting scenes from *Metamorphoses*, by the Roman poet Ovid, first published in English in 1567 and dedicated to Dudley, Earl of Leicester. When Shakespeare started grammar school in Stratford-upon-Avon, Ovid was one of the set texts. If the eleven-year-old boy had been able to sneak into the Privy Garden as Langham had done, he would have enjoyed the imagery as much as any of Elizabeth's courtiers.

THE CECILS AT BURGHLEY, THEOBALDS AND HATFIELD

Elizabeth I's adviser William Cecil (Lord Burghley) and his son Robert were among those who also thought a garden was the way to impress. Burghley House in Northamptonshire, built between 1553 and 1587, had all the latest

The Kenilworth Privy Garden is surrounded by oak trellis. In the centre of each quarter stand 4.5 metre/15 foot-high 'porphyry' obelisks, which are actually wood painted to look like porphyry – a typical Elizabethan device. The marble fountain and aviary were designed to impress.

new arrivals including citrus fruits and pomegranates. Theobalds, one of the Cecil's other houses, was a favourite stopping place for Elizabeth I, a convenient day's ride from London. Here, Burghley created one of the most show-stopping of all Elizabethan gardens. As well as a Privy Garden (containing tulips, lilies and peonies), there was a 2.8 hectare/7 acre Great Garden, which was described in 1598 as having: nine knots, each 21 metres/70 foot square; a mount for better viewing of the knot patterns; a labyrinth or maze; and canals. The gardener responsible for Theobalds (and the Cecils' other house on the Strand) was John Gerard (see page 130).

James I requisitioned Theobalds from Robert Cecil, who had continued his father's legacy, offering him the old palace of Hatfield instead. Robert went on to build Hatfield House, which is the house we see today, although the old palace still exists nearby.

Robert Cecil set about making a Jacobean garden, planting 30,000 vines, 500 cherries (*Prunus*) and 500 mulberries (*Morus*). He used a gardener called Jennings (who had worked at Theobalds) and the hydraulic engineer Salomon de Caus. Caus created a series of terraces to the east of the house, formally laid out with fountains. Beyond this, there was a dell with waterways and an island – perhaps for a banqueting house. There may have been a grotto as there are records of John Tradescant the Elder bringing shells to set in the bed of the stream or on the sides of the walls.

In recent years, Hatfield has been the home of one of the twentieth century's most notable gardeners, the Marchioness of Salisbury. She has been responsible for bring the gardens back to life, reinstating some of the Tudor heritage with a maze and formal gardens. Lady Salisbury instated a knot garden in front of the old palace, while the new house was given a parterre. Box (*Buxus*) and yew (*Taxus*) are used structurally at Hatfield, reflecting the house's Jacobean and later history.

The parterre at Hatfield House in Hertfordshire echoes the 'foot' mazes, which were popular in the early seventeenth century.

The Stratford Boy
Shakespeare's Birthplace

As gardeners do with ordure hide those roots
That shall first spring and be most delicate.

Henry V, Act 2 scene 4

Shakespeare's story begins in the Warwickshire market town of Stratford-upon-Avon. Interestingly, the first documented mention of the Shakespeares in the town was on 29 April 1552, when William's father, John, was fined one shilling for having an unauthorized dung heap in Henley Street. John was from a farming family that raised cattle and sheep, which provided him with the raw material for his trade of glove making. The house he bought in Henley Street a few years later would become his workshop and home to his wife Mary Arden and, in 1564, to his firstborn son, William Shakespeare.

Roses, hollyhocks (*Alcea*) and *Verbascum nigrum* grow in the borders behind Shakespeare's birthplace.
John Shakespeare bought the timber-framed house in 1556, for his new bride Mary Arden.

By 1556, JOHN, WHO HAD SERVED his seven-year apprenticeship and was now described as a glover and whittawer (someone who prepares the leather), had done well enough to buy two houses: a house and garden in Greenhill Street; and, most importantly for this story, a freehold house and garden in Henley Street. The second purchase was most likely to create a home for his new bride, Mary Arden.

In their first five or six years of marriage, John and Mary lost their first two children as infants. This was not uncommon at the time: only one in three Warwickshire children would reach adulthood for a range of reasons. But in the 1560s there was the added threat of the plague. Between the summer of 1563 and the summer of 1564, England suffered the worst outbreak of the disease for the whole sixteenth century. When Mary gave birth to a son, William, in spring 1564, he was baptized quickly – as was the custom – at the Shakespeares' local church, Holy Trinity. It is likely that Mary took the infant to her parents' farm at Wilmcote, to give him the best chance of survival.

LEFT A map of Stratford in 1802 shows the layout of streets, including Henley Street (top right) and Holy Trinity Church (bottom left), where Shakespeare was baptized. The map was collected by Captain James Saunders in the nineteenth century and is known as the Saunders map.
OPPOSITE Holy Trinity Church, Stratford-upon-Avon was the Shakespeare family's church. William was baptized here on 26 April 1564.

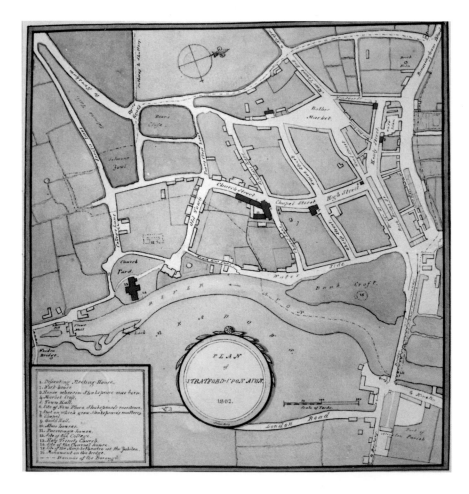

'Bare ruined choirs where late the sweet birds sang'

Sonnet 73

In later life, William Shakespeare would be ridiculed for being the 'upstart crow', the simple, country boy who did not go to university, but, in fact, his father was rather more than just an artisan. Stratford-upon-Avon was a town on the rise – given its town charter by Edward VI on 28 June 1553 shortly before the king was succeeded by Queen Mary and then by Elizabeth I. William would be born into an Elizabethan town where trade, education and social mobility were possible for those with an eye for the opportunities.

John had a somewhat meteoric rise within the local legal and administrative system. He was a juror, constable, assessor of fines and served in the office of chamberlain of the borough in 1562–3 and 1563–4. A year after William was born, John was elected as one of the twelve aldermen of the borough and sat on council meetings and legal proceedings. In 1568, he was bailiff of Stratford and, by the time William was seven, his father was the chief alderman of the town – the equivalent of mayor. John remained a farmer, tanner, glover and wool dealer, yet he managed to weave his business dealings with the duties of town office. In 1575, he was able to buy the adjoining house on Henley Street, including a garden and orchard – the barn of which survived until the late eighteenth century.[1] However, he also seems to have got into debt and become embroiled in several legal disputes – perhaps all part of the cut and thrust of trade in a thriving, sixteenth-century market town. As William Shakespeare grew up, his father was fined several times: for example, for illegal wool dealing and for charging too much interest on a loan.

Over the next ten years, John's position in the Stratford-upon-Avon Corporation declined; his business struggled, he no longer attended meetings and was finally expelled in 1586. He stopped going to church – allegedly to avoid being presented with writs, but possibly because his Catholic sympathies did not sit comfortably with the new Protestantism being enforced by Elizabeth I.

As an official of Stratford-on-Avon Corporation, John had overseen the whitewashing of the wall paintings in the Guild Chapel, which previously had displayed brightly coloured images of biblical stories, purgatory, the murder of Thomas à Becket and the favourite tale of St George and the dragon. The deliberate smashing of the colourful stained glass windows in the chapel on Midsummer Day 1571 was a continuation of this policy. William would have had to grow up quickly. His father's troubles deepened, and the Shakespeares had to mortgage almost all their inherited landholdings – including raising £40 on the property Mary had inherited in Wilmcote. Still later, when his father died in 1601, Shakespeare leased part of the family home to a tenant, Lewis Hiccox, who turned it into a public house, The Swan (later known as The Swan and Maidenhead).

LEFT This painting of 1829 by William Underhill shows the front facade of Shakespeare's house. It was used as an inn and a butcher's shop, but this did not deter visitors wanting to see the place where Shakespeare was born.
BELOW In his time as an official of Stratford-upon-Avon, Shakespeare's father had overseen the whitewashing of wall paintings in the Guild Chapel.

ABOVE AND OPPOSITE The Guildhall
and Guild Chapel were at the heart
of Stratford life during William
Shakespeare's childhood. The school he
attended was in the timbered building
and, as alderman of the borough, his
father, John, would have attended
meetings there.

EDUCATING WILLIAM

It is generally accepted that, because of John's position as a freeholder and
officer of the Corporation of Stratford, William, his eldest son, would have
been able to attend the grammar school from the age of seven free of charge,
although no records exist.

Built in the fourteenth century, the King's New School on Church Street
was a short walk from the Shakespeares' house in Henley Street. It was a high-
status school and the master was paid £20 a year – above average for the time
– and the masters were mainly fellows of the Oxford University colleges. The
curriculum included Latin as the principal subject, and William's familiarity
with the language is shown off in several of his plays including *Love's Labour's
Lost* and *The Merry Wives of Windsor*. Schoolboys of ten or older would have
studied Virgil, Horace and Ovid. There may even have been plays produced
by the boys and performed in Latin. It was an education that encouraged
verbal and written dexterity – ideal grounding for a playwright.

William was aged around eleven or twelve when John and Mary's financial
troubles began. The rocky times may have been the reason that Shakespeare did
not finish his education or go on to university. Yet, William's informal education
was equally as important to the man he became. Stratford-upon-Avon in the
1560s and 1570s was a busy market town of around two thousand inhabitants
– serving the rural communities that surrounded it. William probably travelled
with his father extensively around the Cotswolds, Warwickshire, Gloucestershire
and further afield, buying and selling wool and hides. He was born to country
people living in town – and he never lost this dual identity.

THE OUTSIDE SPACE

William's birthplace at Henley Street is recorded as having a garden, and the
title deeds mention 'orchards'.[2] To imagine the kind of outside space they would
have had, we have to take account of the small-scale industry that was going
on behind the glove-making workshop. Hides were stripped from the animals,
the meat and wool sold on and the tanning process carried out to produce fine
leather goods. There would have been kid, goat, lamb, deer, calf and even dog
carcasses arriving and being dispatched daily; there would have been mounds
of lime and ash for cleaning the skins; clay-lined tanning pits would have been
full of soaking hides; there would be racks for drying the leather and barns for
the storage of hides and wool as well as stabling for horses; and dung heaps.

Despite all this dirty noxious activity, there must still have been a useful
garden for the household, beds for vegetables and essential herbs, and room
for smaller livestock, such as pigs and geese, which could be turned out to feed
in the orchard.

Household Herbs

Here's flowers for you:
Hot lavender, mints, savoury, marjoram,
The Winter's Tale, Act 4 scene 4

While the word 'herb' was used loosely to refer to both wild and cultivated plants, it tended to mean those that were useful in some way. The herbals of sixteenth-century Europe were, in effect, a list of plants as a cure for sickness, those with aromatic properties and those for flavouring food. Thus, what we now think of as herbs – rosemary, marjoram (*Origanum*) and lavender – had a range of uses in the Elizabethan household: in the kitchen as 'pot herbs'; for strewing on the floor for hygiene; and for making cosmetic and remedial potions. Women running an average household, such as Mary Shakespeare at Henley Street, would have grown some of their own in the garden to make into straightforward recipes.

LANGUAGE AND MEANING

There was also an underlying understanding of plants that was commonplace in Shakespeare's lifetime – something all his audience would have understood. Herbs and flowers had a 'language'. In *The Winter's Tale*, the flowers of high summer serve to accentuate Perdita's sense of displacement, and Shakespeare's audience would have known that 'hot' referred to the scientific 'virtue' of the plant. All the herbs would have been in flower and full of aromatic oils under the warm summer sun. In *Hamlet*, Shakespeare has Ophelia, demented by grief, handing out imaginary herbs – each poignant and full of meaning: 'There's rosemary, that's for remembrance. Pray, love, remember.'[3] And, in *Romeo and Juliet*, Friar Laurence, having issued Juliet with the potion that makes her appear dead, instructs the family to put rosemary on the body and carry it to the church 'as the custom is'. The gardener John Gerard notes that rosemary flowers in both spring and autumn. Perhaps its tendency to repeat flower was why it was associated with remembering loved ones. Four centuries later, rosemary often flowers in winter too.

HERBS FOR FIRST AID AND CLEANLINESS

The main household uses for rosemary were as a mouthwash to sweeten the breath, while the flowers were coated with sugar and eaten to 'quicken the spirits and make them more lively'. Distilled lavender water was a common remedy for bathing on the temples for migraines and headaches. Lavender flowers and essences were used for a scented and mildly antiseptic hand wash. An oil extracted from the crushed leaves of marjoram was said to soothe painful joints. Savory – winter and summer (*Satureja hortensis* and *S. montana*) – was made into an ointment for bee and insect stings and could provide an alternative to rosemary in cooking.

Both lavender and rosemary seem to have survived the extreme Elizabethan winters, but sweet marjoram (*Origanum majorana*) was considered tender – Gerard makes a special point of noting that, in the winter of 1597, the leaves of his plant were 'green all this winter long' – something that did not usually happen. It was not unknown for the River Thames in London, where Gerard lived, to freeze for two months at a time.

OPPOSITE, CLOCKWISE FROM TOP LEFT Marjoram; rue; thyme; lemon balm; lavender; mint; and rosemary

After William, John and Mary went on to have five more children – three boys and two girls – named Gilbert, Joan, Anne, Richard and Edmund. The Shakespeares would have employed household servants and apprentices in the business, who occupied the rooms at the top of the house.

Providing for perhaps twelve or more people would have required a constant supply of vegetables and ongoing food preparation on the kitchen fire. The basic diet was bread, ale and potage – a hot soup or stew containing onions, peas, beans, leeks, garlic and herbs from the garden, which could be thickened with cereal and flavoured with meat. Milk, butter, eggs and cheeses would have been readily available at market, and Mary would not have needed to run a dairy in the limited space available at Henley Street. The old town market cross, which stood on the corner of Bridge Street and High Street, might have been the spot where John Shakespeare, and perhaps William too, set up stall to sell their leather goods. Centuries later, the base of that cross would find its way into the new garden at Shakespeare's birthplace.

THE DEVELOPMENT OF THE GARDEN AT HENLEY STREET

The interest in visiting the house where Shakespeare was born began in the 1750s and was fuelled, in part, by David Garrick's revival of the plays in London theatres and his total obsession with everything Shakespearian. On a plan of Stratford published in 1759, the house is clearly marked as 'Shakespeare's birthplace', indicating that it was already on the tourist trail.

There are records in 1762 of a mulberry (*Morus*) tree on the site and, in 1765, of an old walnut (*Juglans*) tree near the back door. Nineteenth-century maps of the town mark out the land behind the birthplace as Guild pits and open fields beyond that, so it is unlikely that the garden was ever much bigger than it is now – around 0.2 hectare/½ acre. By 1800, images show the Swan and Maidenhead and a butcher's shop occupying the building. This rather earthy frontage did not deter visitors, who continued to come in a steady stream. None of them mentions what was going on in the garden so it seems likely that they were not encouraged to look at what was certainly a working backyard.

In 1847, the house and gardens were put up for sale and a national campaign began to save Shakespeare's birthplace for the nation (with notable supporters such as Charles Dickens). At the auction in London on 16 September, £3,000 was paid by a joint London–Stratford committee, which later became the SBT. Dickens, it is thought, bought some of the wooden settles and installed them at his house in Gad's Hill Place, Kent.

The formal layout of the gardens is essentially Victorian with its wide central path and standard hollies (*Ilex*) planted in the 1860s.

The house has a fifteenth-century frame and was once part of a continuous frontage of houses on Henley Street but, in 1857, those either side of the birthplace were demolished, to create a fire barrier. After restoring the interior, the Trust started on the exterior and redesigned the garden, with a formal layout, wide gravel paths, lawns and box (*Buxus*) edging, as well as two prominent cedars of Lebanon (*Cedrus lebani*). The old market cross was erected in the 1860s, and the holly (*Ilex*) hedges planted in the following decade.

In 1861, the SBT received a letter from George Jabet, an amateur gardener and retired solicitor from Handsworth, Birmingham, expressing his dismay that a Shakespearian garden 'does not seem to have been accomplished with much success'.[4] He was so upset that he offered to lend the committee his own books in order to create 'a garden such as a Gentleman of Shakespeare's rank ... would attach to his house'. There are records of an influx of plants in the late Victorian period including dwarf roses, crab apples (*Malus*) and wallflowers (*Erysimum*) – in an attempt to make the garden more 'Shakespearian'.

By the turn of the twentieth century, the garden had matured into one that, more or less, still exists today. It is Victorian, formal and colourful with space for the people to wander at leisure. There was a move towards putting in more Shakespeare-related flowers, and over the next decades there was a general Edwardian emphasis on prettifying the planting.

Each phase of development at the site has opened up a new opportunity for rethinking the garden. In 1928, excavations beside the back wall revealed the foundations of outbuildings – possibly the range of barns that went with the eastern half of the house. In 1964, the works for the building of the new Shakespeare Centre meant that the back wall of the garden needed to be rebuilt and was made higher to keep out the view of the busy Birmingham Road, which runs behind the site. It also allowed for the planting of a new rose bed alongside it.

In 1999–2000, there were six-month-long renovations of the house and garden for the Millennium. The whole question of what period to take the garden 'back' to was again debated. It was agreed that, in Shakespeare's lifetime, it would have been mostly a working yard, and the garden in existence was already 150 years old and still fit for purpose. It therefore made sense to preserve the High Victorian style, with the addition of more herbs and flowers referenced in Shakespeare's plays. David Austen roses, such as *Rosa* Falstaff and *R.* Gentle Hermione, were introduced to represent Shakespearian characters. The pre-war path (which had at some point had a tarmac overlay) was replaced with Yorkstone. The borders were refreshed, and bedding plants near the house kitchen were replaced with herbs. After repeated lopping to remove old branches, the remaining Victorian cedar tree was finally taken down.

'The flowers are sweet, the colours fresh and trim'

Venus and Adonis

The generous borders are edged with turf. In early spring, daffodils (*Narcissus*) and richly coloured primulas appear before the herbaceous plants come into full growth.

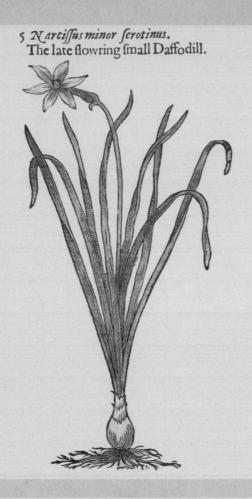

5 *Narciſſus minor ſerotinus.*
The late flowring ſmall Daffodill.

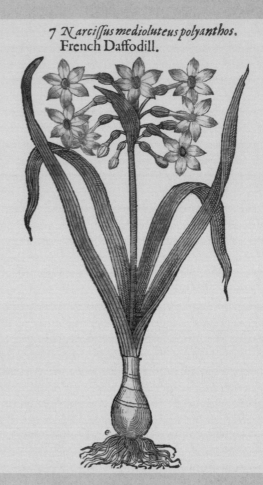

7 *Narciſſus medioluteus polyanthos.*
French Daffodill.

1 *Pſeudonarciſſus luteus multiplex.*
Double yellow Daffodill.

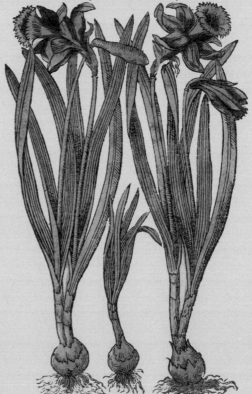

2 *Pſeudonarciſſus Anglicus & Hiſpanicus.*
Common yellow Daffodilly.

Daffodils

When daffodils begin to peer,
With heigh, the doxy over the dale,
Why then comes in the sweet o' the year,
The Winter's Tale, Act 4 scene 3

The native daffodil (*Narcissus*) Shakespeare would have known is *N. pseudonarcissus*, which is happiest in damp meadows and woodland edges. In the twenty-first century, it is increasingly rare but the best displays in the wild are still in Gloucestershire – the neighbouring county to Warwickshire. The woodland margins and meadows beside the River Avon, the River Stour and the Shottery Brook by Anne Hathaway's Cottage are all locations in which Shakespeare could have seen wild daffodils growing as a boy and as a man. His contemporary John Gerard confirms that 'the common wilde daffodil growth wilde in fields and sides of woods in the west parts of England'.

The name daffodil has its origin in the Old English word affodyle; this means 'that which comes early' and can be traced back to the Latin *asphodelus* and the Greek *asphodelos*. By the twelfth century, writers were mentioning it as a good flower to grow in gardens. The most widely used name for the wild daffodil in Warwickshire and elsewhere was the Lent lily, because of its propensity to be out before Easter in Britain. *Narcissus pseudonarcissus* is still one of the most perfectly formed of all the daffodils, being neither diminutive nor overblown, and its corona and tepals are perfectly in balance.

For Shakespeare, the daffodil seems to represent his past – his 'spring' – and in *The Winter's Tale* he relates the Roman myth of Proserpina, in which the lilies of the field turn to daffodils as they fall to earth, expressing a sadness for passing youth.

When he was writing *The Winter's Tale* in the winter of 1609, he was already forty-five years old. He was probably back home in Stratford-upon-Avon and his thoughts were turning to youth, the yearning for a long winter to end, and the coming of spring. Perdita is hosting a feast of sheep shearing and welcomes her guests with flowers. But they are the wrong flowers – they are the 'hot' flowers of middle summer and middle age, not of youth:

I would I had some flowers o'th' spring that might
Become your time of day . . . daffodils,
That come before the swallow dares, and take
The winds of March with beauty
The Winter's Tale, Act 4 scene 4

ABOVE *Narcissus pseudonarcissus*
OPPOSITE Daffodil illustrations from John Gerard's *Herball* of 1597

THE GARDEN TODAY

For many people from around the world, the first experience of trying to connect with Shakespeare will be at his house and garden in Henley Street. After coming out from the illuminated, state-of-the-art exhibition space, visitors get their first glimpse of the ancient building and its garden.

The aim is to keep this as the high-status garden that was laid out in the nineteenth century, so the parallel grass borders edging the double herbaceous border have been reinstated. The planting is constantly replaced and upgraded. As these are the first borders that visitors see, the aim is for high impact and a long season of interest, beginning with a jewel-like display of tulips in spring and continuing with herbaceous planting for summer and autumn.

The garden is divided by a wide, north–south stone path flanked by a double herbaceous border, interspersed with standard roses along its length. One side is backed by a hedge of holly, with standard holly 'lollipops' emerging from its bulk. Herbs are included in the western part of the garden to show the range of species that Shakespeare's mother would have grown for domestic use.

A dwarf yew (*Taxus*) hedge around the terrace area directs visitors towards the side door of the house. The garden immediately abutting the walls of the building has undergone many incarnations – the latest is a parterre of heathers (*Calluna*) sweeping up to the building. Using the different textures and colours of *C. vulgaris* cultivars such as 'Allegro', 'Firefly' and 'Wickwar Flame', this is an oblique reference to the Scottish heath where the witches gather in *Macbeth*.[5] Wild heaths and heathers did exist in the sixteenth century, although rarely as garden plants. They rose to popularity in the Victorian era, and this trend continued into the 1960s, when the Shakespeare Centre was built, and beyond.

The eastern half of the garden, known as the Fairy Lawn, has been left as open grass, and it doubles as an outdoor 'players' space in summer. The garden team are always aware that this is a high foot-fall garden. It needs to be accessible, to allow a flow of people through it and to be arresting – hence the high numbers of brightly coloured perennials and roses. The High Victorian formality, while being light years away from the muddied yard and simple beds of John Shakespeare's time, is a successful choice for a garden that has close to a million pairs of feet walking through it every year.

RIGHT Leaded windows overlook the Yorkstone path, which was laid to accommodate the growing numbers of visitors wanting to see the place where Shakespeare was born.
OVERLEAF Among the roses are those with Shakespearian names, including *Rosa* Falstaff, *R.* Gentle Hermione and *R.* William Shakespeare 2000.

ABOVE In summer, the borders gain height with hollyhocks (*Alcea*), verbascums and white shasta daisies (*Leucanthemum × superbum*).

OPPOSITE, CLOCKWISE FROM TOP LEFT *Rosa* 'Dearest'; lavender (*Lavendula angustifolia*); good King Henry (*Chenopodium bonus-henricus*); *Rosa* 'Allgold'; southernwood (*Artemisia abrotanum*); bladder campion (*Silene vulgaris*); and bear's breeches (*Acanthus spinosus*).

FUTURE GENERATIONS

The house at Henley Street continued to be a major part of Shakespeare's life. When he married Anne Hathaway at the age of eighteen, the couple probably set up home in the two-roomed western part of the house. Their daughter Susanna was born in 1583, and the twins, Judith and Hamnet, started life here two years later. In fact, everything suggests that this was Shakespeare's 'home away from London' until he purchased New Place at the age of thirty-three (see page 157). His parents certainly lived on at Henley Street until the death of John Shakespeare in 1601. Mary died in 1606 and might have moved into New Place as a widow. William, as the eldest son, inherited the Henley Street property and his sister Joan lived on in part of it (for a rent of twelve pence a year) until the middle of the seventeenth century. It then passed to Shakespeare's granddaughter, Elizabeth, and although it was no longer used as a house it stayed in family ownership until the early nineteenth century.

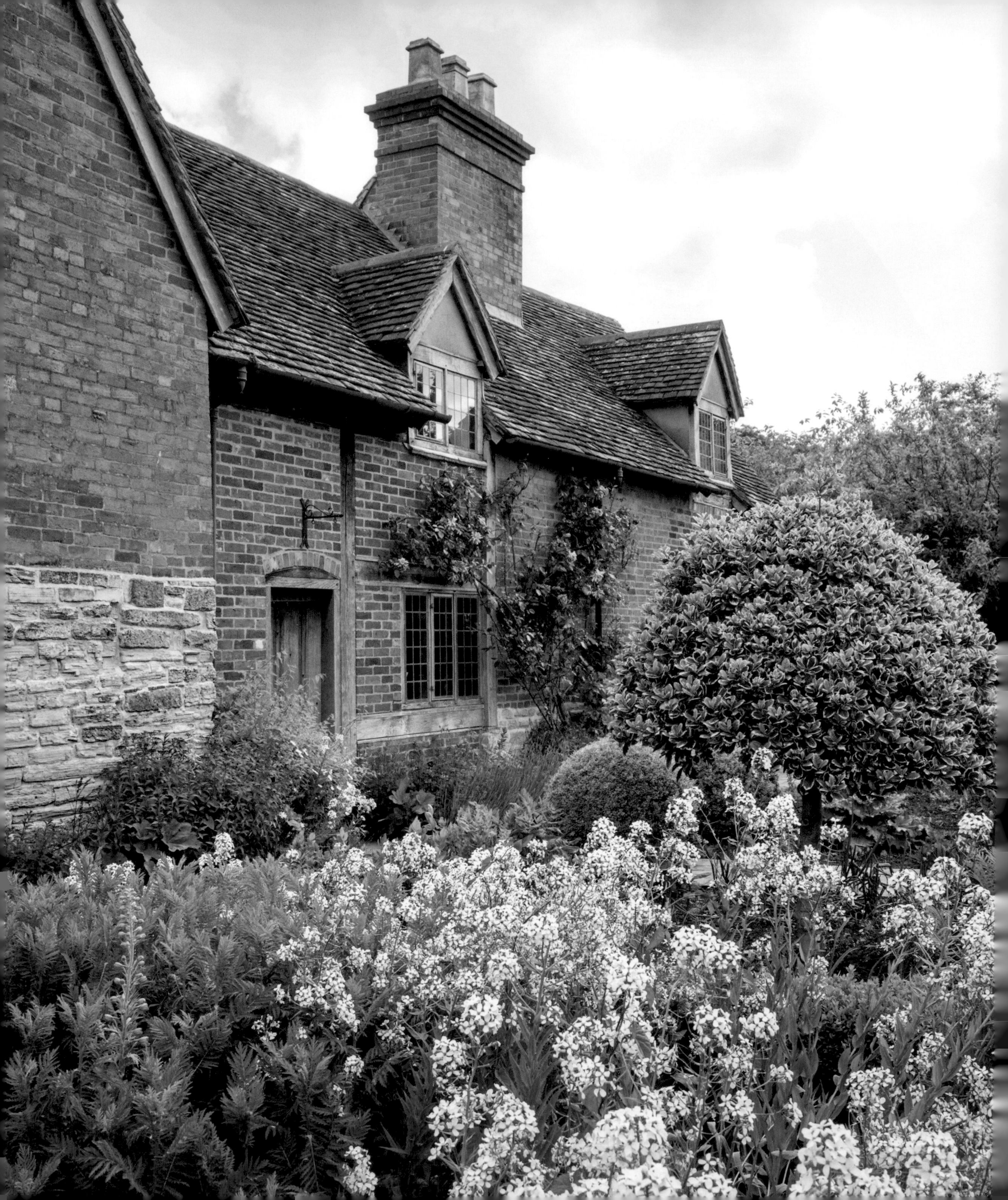

A Country Childhood
Mary Arden's Farm

The strawberry grows underneath the nettle,
And wholesome berries thrive and ripen best
Neighboured by fruit of baser quality;

Henry V, Act 1 scene 1

Shakespeare's affinity for botany came not from his education and
reading but from his upbringing in Warwickshire, and especially
from time he spent at his mother's home. In this chapter of our story,
women are at the heart of Shakespeare's rural roots and family.
The hamlet of Wilmcote lies 5 kilometres/3 miles to the north-west of
Stratford-upon-Avon in the parish of Aston Cantlow, within an area
known as the Forest of Arden. Shakespeare's grandfather,
Robert Arden, built a house here in the year 1514 and had eight
daughters, the youngest of whom was Mary.

Old-fashioned cottage-garden plants are now a feature of the garden surrounding the house where Shakespeare's
mother was born. The borders include white phlox and clipped variegated hollies (*Ilex*) for structure.

ROBERT WAS A SUBSTANTIAL FARMER with a team of eight oxen and seven cows – a mixed farm of crops and dairy production. The household would have brewed its own beer, and made malt from the barley. There was a sizeable vegetable garden and orchard to feed the household, as well as pigs and poultry to rear. The gruelling, year-round calendar would have included sowing, harrowing, ploughing, dunging the land, mowing and gathering up the cut hay to make into stooks or ricks for drying, as well as mucking out the stables and barns.

Mary, it seems, was special to Robert, for when he died in December 1556 he named the sixteen-year-old Mary as his executor – an indication that she was bright and could probably read and possibly write. He bequeathed her a substantial sum of money (£6 13s 6d) and 'all my land in Willmecote called Asbyes and the crop upon the grounde, sowne and tilled as it is'. Asbyes consisted of 28 hectares/70 acres of arable land and 6.5 hectares/16 acres of meadow in Wilmcote and was where Mary and John Shakespeare would later build a house for their tenants.

It could well have been the inheritance from her father that prompted Mary Arden to marry John Shakespeare a year or so later. Mary and John may have met during negotiations over the land in Snitterfield that Robert leased to the Shakespeares. As executor, Mary Arden would have had responsibilities to her father's tenants, and she retained strong ties to her village and the Arden land.

LEGEND AND REALITY – THE FOREST OF ARDEN

> They say he is already in the Forest of Ardenne,
> and a many merry men with him; and there they live
> like the old Robin Hood of England. They say many
> young gentlemen flock to him every day, and fleet the
> time carelessly, as they did in the golden world.
> *As You Like It*, Act 1 scene 1

The main action in *As You Like It* is set in the Forest of Ardenne. Although Shakespeare based his play on an existing romance, *Rosalynde* by Thomas Lodge, it is still hard to ignore the connection with the Warwickshire Forest of Arden that he knew.

Robin Hood is one of the many medieval legends that Shakespeare would have grown up with. There was also Guy of Warwick, the Saxon hero who, after fighting the Danes and the Saracens, retired to the Forest of Arden to

Despite its nineteenth-century exterior, the central part of Mary Arden's House has been dated to 1514.

become a hermit. These are the stories – along with George and the dragon and other heroic tales – that were featured in the books read aloud to children, and were depicted on wall hangings and cloths in Tudor houses. It would be enough to fire the imagination of a young boy, listening to the stories of his grandmother, mother and aunts at the Ardens' farm.

Shakespeare never knew his maternal grandfather, but Robert was distantly related to the Ardens of Park Hall in Cudworth about 30 kilometres/19 miles north-east of Stratford-upon-Avon. Park Hall was a focus for religious dissent and, in the 1580s, Edward Arden was arrested for his alleged part in the Somerville plot to kill Elizabeth I. He was later held in the Tower of London, tortured and finally hung at London's Smithfield. Arden was supposed to have kept a Catholic priest at Park Hall, disguised as a gardener. This was a story being played out throughout Warwickshire, although whether Mary ever visited Park Hall is not known.

The actual boundaries and status of the Forest of Arden, however, remain an enigma. It is a high plateau, overlooking the Avon valley, but it was never part of a royal forest, although it does seem to have had special status.[1] Its reputation today rests more on Shakespeare than on reality, but as a real place it appeared in a 1088 cartulary of Abingdon Abbey, when one Turkill de Eardene adopted the name of the district. It became known as 'free Arden', that is, as a place not under the usual forest laws, which would have restricted hunting to the noble classes.[2] By the twelfth century, it was being used as a loose description of the area, and the first reference to 'forest' was in 1148, when Robert Ferrars Early gave all his 'forest of Arden' to Mervale Abbey – this may have meant, simply, his woodland rather than a forest with hunting rights. By 1221, it seems to have had its own customary rights, with people being allowed to build and put up hedges and banks on common pastureland.

Under Henry VIII, woodland was under pressure for building houses and ships, and there were timber shortages. Therefore, in 1544, a Royal Act was passed to say that, if you owned a wood of less than twenty-four years' growth, you must leave twelve oaks (*Quercus*), elm (*Ulmus*), ash (*Fraxinus*) or beech (*Fagus*) as standing trees. Perhaps this ensured that parts of the plateau remained wooded. Whatever the reality of Arden, it is not hard to believe how its story – of free men and free hunting, where animals that strayed into wooded areas would be without the law – might have appealed to the romantic imagination of a free-thinking playwright.

Austy Wood, near Henley-on-Arden, with its bluebells (*Hyacinthoides non-scripta*) and light tree canopy is a typical small Warwickshire woodland. The term 'arden' relates to a particular topography: a steep or high wooded plateau.

ABOVE In spring, the new lambs and sheep are allowed to graze in the old orchard of apple trees.

OPPOSITE Rare and local breeds such as the Tamworth pig are raised on Mary Arden's Farm, which is run according to organic principles.

THE TUDOR FARMING LANDSCAPE

In John Leland's *Itinerary* of 1540, he found Warwickshire north of the River Avon: 'much enclosed, plentiful of grass, but no great plenty of corn'.[3] This was the period when Mary Arden was growing up at Wilmcote, and it was predominantly a pastoral landscape. Farms such as the Ardens' would have had their team of oxen, a couple of horses, sheep and a few dairy cows for their own consumption. Two-thirds of the land would be pasture and perhaps one-third arable – comprising crops such as rye, barley, oats, wheat and peas.[4]

The Ardens' farm was large for the time– more than 40 hectares/100 acres – so we might call Robert Arden a yeoman rather than a husbandman. There would have been a small outbuilding for storing grain (there is still a granary attached to Mary Arden's farm), a dairy (with a churn, skimmer and cheese press), a cart shed and a range of outbuildings for animals, including a pigsty. The rotation system (known as 'up-and-down farming') would put land to plough for two or three years and then leave it as pasture for grazing for fifteen to twenty years.

'Gives not the
hawthorn bush
a sweeter shade
To shepherds
looking on their
seely sheep'

Henry VI Part III,
Act 2 scene 5

The Ardens ran a mixed farm, with sheep, cattle and other livestock. Iron shears that could be sharpened were a multipurpose tool used for wool shearing and for general garden work.

WOMEN'S ROLES

The play *As You Like It*, which is set in the Forest of Ardenne, brings us closest to the country life of the young William Shakespeare, which was one run by women. After Robert's death, his wife Agnes, along with her daughters – Shakespeare's mother Mary and her seven sisters and half-sisters – would continue to work the farm. They may have employed male day labourers, but it seems likely that Agnes and the daughters would have done a lot of the work themselves. As well as the farm and household work, they were already running the gardens, the dairy, the brewhouse and the 'still' (the distilling of various plants for 'waters' including lavender, rose and rosemary for washing, disinfecting and cleaning).

Women were responsible for weeding – in the garden and in the fields. This applied to removing weeds and to collecting weeds (or herbs), which were delivered to apothecaries and for which payment would be made. In the gardens at York Place in London (which would become Whitehall), twenty-two women were employed at 3d a day.[5] In 1530, women were employed at the Oxford colleges for the same wage.

Many illustrations of the period show women working in gardens – pushing wheelbarrows and tending vegetables. Books for the 'hus'wife' and 'hus'band' included Fitzherbert's *The Book of Husbandry* – first published in 1523 and still being updated in 1598. Fitzherbert's book was for the literate country gentleman or woman rather than for labourers. It contained advice on ploughing with oxen, how to sow barley and oats, how to make tools and plant trees. This would soon be joined by the bestselling, self-improvement handbook by Thomas Tusser (see panel, opposite).

There are records of women taking on paid roles outside the farm or household, on larger estates. At Charlecote Park a few kilometres from Shakespeare's home, Agnes Eaton is recorded as the maltster, in 1572 – the year Queen Elizabeth came to visit Sir Thomas Lucy. The pertinently named Ales Brewer was one of several women employed by Henry VIII at Hampton Court – Ales supplied the garden with strawberry plants, which presumably she grew herself or collected from the wild.[6]

THE DEVELOPMENT OF THE FARM AND GARDEN

Mary Arden's Farm today occupies around 28 hectares/70 acres in the north-east of Wilmcote. There are two houses on the site and, until 2000, it was thought that the sixteenth-century timbered house known as Palmer's Farm was the Arden home. However, research commissioned by the SBT in 2000 has revealed that Mary Arden's was actually the house next door – then called Glebe Farm.[7]

Thomas Tusser and the Art of Husbandry

May
Watch bees in May
For swarming away
Both now and in June
Marke maister bees tune.
Thomas Tusser (1573)

Thomas Tusser's practical manual of country life contained everything someone running a smallholding in sixteenth-century Britain might need to know, from pig feeding to laying out a garden. It was aimed squarely at the hus'band and hus'wife, and the first edition was published in English in 1557 as *A Hundredth Good Pointes of Husbandrie*. The thing that made it so memorable was that the text was written in rhyme. This meant that if there was one literate person in the household, they could recite the rhymes to others. It was so successful that it was enlarged to become *Five Hundred Pointes of Good Husbandrie* (1573) and was never out of print for two hundred years.

Tusser was born in Essex c.1524 and educated at Trinity College, Cambridge. He returned to country life, to Suffolk, to become a farmer at Cattawade near the River Stour in the 1550s. His books are written from first-hand knowledge, and he does not use the usual classical references of earlier manuals, which were translated from Latin or Greek.

The roles of husbandman and housewife are clearly defined. The housewife is instructed with the tasks of brewing, malting, cleaning, scouring, baking and dairy work, while the husbandman must take advice on everything from ploughing to barley sowing and cutting peasticks.

The 'garden' in a sixteenth-century country household is part of the farm – there is really no distinction. That said, Tusser does mention knots and borders and emphasizes neatness – the look of the plot was important. He also gives us a good list of tools that were used: rake, mattock, spade, dibble (dibber), line and level.

Hedges are mentioned but their main use seems to be for drying washing on. Shakespeare also refers to this in *The Winter's Tale* when Autolycus the tinker sings of 'the white sheet bleaching on the hedge'.[8] Tusser's list of vegetables is also enlightening. There are broad beans, cabbages and 'runcival' peas (rotund – probably marrowfat) and turnips and carrots to 'boile or butter'. In all, he lists thirty types of fruit and soft fruit, and 170 other plants, either to eat, to strew on the floor or to grow in windows and pots.

The frontispiece for the 1599 edition of Thomas Tusser's
Five Hundred Pointes of Good Husbandrie

It is easy to see how the mistake happened. Palmer's Farm is a good-looking, timber-framed house of roughly the right period (it is actually a few years out – it was built in 1569–81, fifteen or twenty years after Mary inherited). When, in the 1880s, Shakespeare followers began to take an interest in where his mother had been born, it looked a more suitable candidate than the rather plain, 'modern'-looking, brick-fronted building further down the road. There was even a pretty garden. James Walter in *Shakespeare's True Life* (1890) describes how much he enjoyed 'the flowers in the garden, the stonecrop on the garden wall'.[9] When the SBT bought the property in the 1930s, all that was needed was a light tidy-up, clipping the box (*Buxus*) hedges and replanting country flowers of the region.

Mary Arden's true house has now been dated to 1514. The farm, at four-and-a-half yardlands (approximately 55 hectares/135 acres), was the largest landholding in the village, sitting at the south end of a plot of land or 'croft', which would have consisted of house, garden, farmyard, outbuildings and open field to the north.[10] The house is part brick, part stone, part timber-framed, with a red-clay tile roof, and it forms part of a rectangular range of farm buildings – a granary, pigsty, barns and open cart sheds.

The well in the garden is one of several discovered by the Shakespeare Birthplace Trust when they bought Mary Arden's House in 1968.

It was serendipity that the SBT bought the house in 1968 to save it from development, unaware that it was the birthplace of Shakespeare's mother. The garden was wild and devoid of features apart from two wells and handsome blue lias stone walls with coping to the south and west boundaries. The garden was laid out in typical country fashion with local random paving, herbaceous plants, shrubs, gooseberry bushes and herbs, while climbing roses were set against the house.

The other buildings on the site, such as the dovecote and cider house, began to be shown to the public. Gradually, over the intervening years, the land has been developed so that Mary Arden's Farm today encompasses four adjoining 'crofts' running north–south to meet the road at the front, from the east; these are known as The Rickyard, Palmer's Croft, Falconer's Field and Mary Arden's Croft. At the north end, the medieval ridge and furrows of the open field system are still visible, preserved in earthworks. A conservation plan has been put into action that celebrates Warwickshire's Tudor country heritage – with demonstrations of hedge-laying and traditional ploughing, falconry, flocks of Cotswold sheep and Longhorn cattle, working horses, and rare breeds of pigs and poultry. It also builds on the wildlife value of the site with a new native flower meadow and butterfly banks.

THE GARDENS TODAY

Mary Arden's Farm is run as a working farm with Soil Association organic status, and the garden plots are part of the wider picture of Tudor food production. The site includes a puddled clay wildlife pond, with an island of self-seeded alders (*Alnus*) and willow (*Salix*), where grass snakes, coots and moorhens nest. Mature plum (*Prunus domestica*) and cherry (*P. avium*) trees stand in Falconer's Field and sheep graze in the apple orchard above Palmer's Croft, where rabbits and even muntjac deer are welcomed (or at least not deterred).

The circular dung heap is used to demonstrate the Tudor method of layering straw bedding with animal manure and household waste, to produce a natural soil improver.

There is a very visible midden (dung heap) in the middle of the farmyard – a vital part of the whole livestock–manure–food cycle on the farm. The midden consists of layers of raked-up animal dung and bedding straw, plus household waste. Pigs, chickens and geese roam freely, and all the fencing around the site is made from local hand-cleft oak.

Palmer's Farm was a substantial yeoman's house and the beds in front of it, being visible from the road, would have been decorative. The beds are edged with reused handmade tiles and filled with herbs and flowers: rosemary, pot marigolds (*Calendula*), roses, cowslips (*Primula veris*) and scented plants. Against the house, roses and climbing peas (*Lathyrus grandiflorus*) scramble up the walls. The underlying bedrock is lias limestone, overlain with clay, so this is not the easiest garden plot to dig.

Around Mary Arden's House the beds are planted each year with useful herbs and vegetables, to help visitors understand the range of Tudor plants available.

The front garden of Palmer's Farm reuses old tiles for edging and is planted with pot marigolds (*Calendula*), a standard rosemary and chives.

RIGHT Under the windows of the house, the scrambling pea *Lathyrus grandiflorus* is allowed free rein.

OPPOSITE, CLOCKWISE FROM TOP LEFT *Thalictrum* 'Splendide White'; *Rosa* 'Henri Martin'; pot marigold (*Calendula officinalis*); *Bergenia* 'Silberlicht'; chives; *Rosa canina* 'Andersonii'; and *Salvia nemerosa*.

A couple of variegated standard hollies (*Ilex*) have been retained, beneath which are grown rows of caraway, dill, garlic, parsnips, onions, carrots, radishes and corn salad. There is a semi-permanent planting of dye plants – madder (*Rubia tinctorum*), woad (*Isatis tinctoria*) and weld (*Reseda luteola*) – although dyes were not usually made at home. Cloth would be professionally dyed by members of the craftsmen's guild in Stratford-upon-Avon, and a busy housewife would not have had time for such tasks. A small circular area – known as the 'wise woman's garden' – is used to grow the kind of things that Mary Arden, her mother and grandmother might have needed: mullein (*Verbascum*), bugle (*Ajuga*), clary sage (*Salvia sclarea*), sweet Cicely (*Myrrhis odorata*), self-heal (*Prunella vulgaris*), lungwort (*Pulmonaria officinalis*), valerian (*Valeriana officinalis*), chamomile (*Chamaemelum nobile*) and other easily grown ingredients for home remedies.

Recent additions to the gardens are the Tudor-style vegetable plots between the two farmhouses. Each plot is enclosed with woven willow hurdles, and

OPPOSITE Yellow tansy (*Tanacetum vulgare*) was one of the herbs recommended for strewing by the writer Thomas Tusser, possibly for its insecticidal properties.

BELOW The kitchen garden beds around Mary Arden's house include climbing runner beans and purple cabbages.

the rectangular beds are used for alexanders (*Smyrnium olusatrum*), onions, leeks, garlic, lovage (*Levisticum*), strawberry spinach (*Chenopodium capitatum*), skirret (*Sium sisarum*) and kale. Skirrets look rather like tall (1.2 metre/4 foot) cow parsley (*Anthriscus sylvestris*) in flower, but it is the root that interested the Tudors. Its long 'fingers' took 2–3 years to bulk up and then half the root would be chopped away to be added to the pot, while the rest was left in the ground to increase again. As the crop could be eaten in a single sitting, it was not particularly economic. Alexanders were a multipurpose vegetable. The young leaves, which often survive the winter, are hot and peppery, and the flower buds were also eaten as well as the seeds.

The beds are composted with the farm's home-made compost, and no chemicals are used anywhere on the land. The beds are planted in succession to make sure there is not a glut of one type of crop. All the produce is used by the interpretation staff, who work daily in Palmer's farmhouse, cooking food

BELOW The Tudor beds are laid out in rectangles and contain plants such as nasturtiums and pot marigolds (*Calendula*) for household use.

OPPOSITE, CLOCKWISE FROM TOP LEFT Salsify (with seed head); wild rocket (in flower); lovage; asparagus peas (in flower); endive; borage; and adjacent plantings of beetroot and carrots.

Food in Tudor Times

Tudor citizens ate well, particularly on the country farms. There were cattle for beef, sheep for mutton, small birds such as capons and pigeon and the meats of hunting – venison, partridge, pheasant, hare and rabbit. Birds and fowl were fed on specific plants in order to the flavour the meat: for example, rosemary and pennyroyal (*Mentha pulegium*) – a strongly flavoured wild mint. Capons were fed on *Lychnis* seeds (known as cockle).

At the town markets there would be cheeses for sale, fresh river fish (or salted sea fish), as well as bread made from rye or wheat flour. In cities such as London there were oysters and shellfish and spices such as saffron, nutmeg and cloves. The Tudors were fond of pies and pastries; sugar was widely available but expensive, and, in rural areas, honey was more commonly used. Prince Hal is handed a pennyworth of sugar in a London tavern, in *Henry IV Part I*.[11] Sugared or candied flowers and roots were popular as snacks – particularly *oringo*, the candied root of the sea holly (*Eryngium maritimum*).

EDIBLE VEGETABLES

According to the agricultural historian Joan Thirsk, the greatest change in Shakespeare's age was the eating of more vegetables and herbs.[12] To feed the workers and the family, they would have needed a garden stocked with vegetables for the pottage: cabbages (or 'coles'), leeks, carrots, onions, turnips, peas and beans, particularly broad and kidney beans. The herbalist William Turner notes that: 'persnepes [parsnips] and skirwortes [skirret] are common in England'.[13] Skirret (*Sium sisarum*) is a root vegetable – the long white roots had been added to the pot long before potatoes were known in Britain.

Potatoes had been discovered in Peru, and by the latter part of the sixteenth century Sir Walter Raleigh had brought them back from Virginia and North Carolina and was growing them on his estates in Ireland. The story is that, when he presented them to Elizabeth I,

her cook used only the leaves, throwing away the tubers. When Falstaff says: 'Let the sky rain potatoes',[14] he is clearly thinking of them as a luxury item, as well as an aphrodisiac. They certainly did not become anything like a staple vegetable until centuries later.

The rising interest in vegetables can probably be put down to the number of holy days and saints days of fasting, which meant eating only fish or vegetables. Such fasting was undertaken for the whole of forty days of Lent, from Ash Wednesday to Easter Sunday. These religious festivals became less numerous after the Reformation in the mid-sixteenth century, but certainly would have been a normal part of family life for Shakespeare's mother and grandparents.

SALLETS [SALADS]

Vegetables were grown near the house and were a staple foodstuff; for poorer households, they were almost the only food. 'Sallet' was a generic name for plants grown for eating and were distinguished from 'herbs', which had a specific use. In reality, a 'sallet' was a mix of herbs, vegetables and what we would today call salad crops – radishes and lettuce – all dressed with oil, vinegar and sugar. Globe artichokes were also commonly grown in kitchen gardens; they had been cultivated by the Romans in Britain and had a revival in the mid-sixteenth century.

John Evelyn, writing a century later, divides salads into those to be eaten uncooked (including purslane and rocket) and those to be lightly cooked (including endive, cabbage and lettuces).

OPPOSITE, CLOCKWISE FROM TOP LEFT White cabbage (cole); garden radish; red strawberry; and garden colewort

and making cosmetic preparations such as bowls of lavender-water handwash and rosemary hairwash.

Herbs are collected from the gardens and dried naturally from the rafters. Root vegetables are piled up and stored over winter – country people would have supplemented the dried peas and beans kept in winter store with nettle-tops (*Urtica*) foraged from the hedgerow in early spring. The Tudors had a huge range of flavoured vinegars (malt vinegar being a by-product of making beer) and used them to pickle cucumbers, cabbages and root vegetables.

THE ARDEN HERITAGE

As an adult, Shakespeare would draw more and more on the memories of his mother's house. By the time he wrote *As You Like It* (performed at the Globe in early 1600) he was in his mid-thirties and had already bought his own house in Stratford-upon-Avon. After making London his home for ten or more years, he was keen to forge links again with his native Warwickshire. He even gave a small part to a character called William (a 'countryman' in the plot), who has 'wit' (intelligence) and who hails from the Forest of Arden.[15] When Shakespeare writes so artlessly of farming, rural life and wild flowers, we can feel the country boy emerging once again. Yet this may have been more to do with the fact that this childhood world was no longer 'his'.

In 1577, when John and Mary Shakespeare were struggling with debts, they mortgaged part of the Arden holdings to Edmund Lambert, Mary's brother-in-law. When they tried to retrieve it, the Lamberts refused. It was another family dispute that rumbled on for two decades. In the late 1590s, during the last few years of John's life, William would try to help his parents to win back the land. You can see why it would have been important to him to reclaim his mother's own piece of the Forest of Arden. Their suit to reclaim the land was unsuccessful, but his quest to make his father (and himself) a gentleman with a coat of arms (a cause that was strengthened by the connection with the Arden family) would succeed in 1596, with the motto 'Non sanz droict' ('Not without right').

'My salad days,
When I was green in
judgment'

Antony and Cleopatra,
Act 1 scene 5

The 'wise woman's garden' contains a complete household cabinet of useful plants including wormwood (*Artemisia absinthium*), self-heal (*Prunella vulgaris*), peonies, roses, chamomile (*Chamaemelum nobile*) and great mullein (*Verbascum thapsus*).

Youth and Romance
Anne Hathaway's Cottage

Yet marked I where the bolt of Cupid fell.
It fell upon a little western flower –
Before, milk-white; now, purple with love's wound –
And maidens call it love-in-idleness.

A Midsummer Night's Dream, Act 2 scene 1

Everyone loves a love story and Shakespeare's has all the romance
befitting a poet. In the summer of 1582, William, aged eighteen, met
Anne Hathaway, whose family farmed in the village of Shottery,
just west of his home in Stratford-upon-Avon. Although the families
knew each other, exactly how the couple met remains a mystery.
Nevertheless, what followed on from their courtship ensured that
Anne Hathaway's Cottage, and particularly its garden surrounding
the thatched homestead, would be forever associated with
William Shakespeare.

Anne Hathaway's birthplace has become one of the most famous
houses and gardens associated with the playwright.

'With April's first-born flowers, and all things rare'

Sonnet 21

Blue and white *Anemone blanda* appear beneath the trees each spring.

ANNE WAS TWENTY-SIX, the oldest daughter of the household. In late August 1582, William Shakespeare might have been helping the Hathaways with the harvest – and the merrymaking that followed. That certainly would be around the right date to tie in with the birth, nine months later of Anne and William's baby girl, Susanna.

Anne's father had died the previous year, leaving a dowry for Anne of ten marks (£6 13s 4d) – the usual portion at the time. In November 1582, a special licence was issued by the bishop of Worcester to allow William and Anne to marry, and two Shottery farmers agree to pay a bond of £40 if the marriage did not go ahead. Despite many different interpretations of why a special licence was needed, the facts are that Anne was three months' pregnant at the time of the marriage and William was under the age of consent, which was twenty-one. We do not know where they were married and over the years various churches have tried to claim the privilege.

HISTORY OF THE FARM

The house and land now known as Anne Hathaway's Cottage (then called Hewlands) was held in the mid-sixteenth century by Anne's grandfather, John Hathaway, from the manor of Old Stratford. It consisted then of two houses – one with a yardland of open field (approximately 12 hectares/30 acres), the other with one and half yardlands (18 hectares/45 acres) and three 'closes' (which were enclosed parcels of land). When Anne's father died, his widow Joan and her daughters carried on the farming business there until the late 1590s. Like the Ardens' farm in Wilmcote, the Hathaways' was a farm run largely by women – Anne's brother Bartholomew was eventually able to buy the freehold of the farm in 1610.

Anne Hathaway, with her mother and siblings, raised pigs, cattle, sheep and poultry and worked the open fields, tilling, ploughing and harvesting oats, barley and wheat. They would have taken produce to market in Stratford-upon-Avon (another plausible meeting place for Anne and William). Anne would have been running the dairy, milking the cows, gathering up the hay and weeding in the fields as well as raising poultry and growing vegetables and herbs for the kitchen. We know there was an orchard beyond the house, but what we now see as a garden was then a working farmyard, with barns, hayricks and dung heaps as well as geese, chickens and dogs foraging around for scraps.

The house sits perpendicular to the village road, which runs alongside a stream known as Shottery Brook. The central part of the thatched, timber-framed building we see today is the oldest, and has an oak cruck frame dendro-dated to 1462 or 1463. It sits on a limestone plinth with wattle-and-daub partitions forming the walls within. It was extended to the west in the

ABOVE This British School painting dates from the mid-nineteenth century, when the Hathaways' home began its transformation from a working farm to a picturesque cottage.

OPPOSITE The garden designer Ellen Willmott suggested the box (*Buxus*) topiary in the borders. *Kerria japonica* has been planted just inside the oak gate.

seventeenth century and has been repaired at various stages, but remains in essence a late medieval farmhouse. Inside are many pieces of furniture that would have belonged to the Hathaways, including a courting chair carved with Shakespeare's shield.

FROM FARMYARD TO COTTAGE GARDEN

So, how did a working farmyard become one of the world's best-known cottage gardens? In many ways, the transformation of Anne Hathaway's Cottage encapsulates the rise of interest in cottage gardening and the way working plots gradually became more decorative. Before the eighteenth century, there is very little evidence of what we would now think of as a cottage garden – with flowers, fruit and vegetables mingled artfully together.

In Tudor times, if a poor cottager had any land at all for their own use that was not given over to keeping a pig or hens, it would have been dedicated to growing something edible – a patch of beans, cabbages or onions – and perhaps

'You see, sweet maid, we marry
A gentler scion to the wildest stock,'

The Winter's Tale,
Act 4 scene 4

some medicinal herbs. Nevertheless, flowers crept in by way of people digging something interesting up from the hedgerows or fields and nurturing it in their garden: a piece of honeysuckle (*Lonicera*) or old man's beard (*Clematis vitalba*) perhaps, or a runner taken from a wild strawberry (*Fragaria*) that had larger than usual berries. This is how wild plants became selected for gardens. Landowners with more resources could develop their gardens by employing gardeners and buying plants from nurseries or swapping them with other garden owners.

The Hathaways are listed as having a 'toft', which, being distinct from the open fields and the 'closes', could indicate a garden plot. The house stayed in the family for the next 250 years, although, by the end of the seventeenth century, much of the land had been sold off. The Hathaways lived in only part of the house and rented out the rest, turning it effectually into two, and later three, cottages. In 1828, it was sold to a Thomas Barnes, and it is from the 1820s that we get the earliest views of the house with its dilapidated barn and what would become the garden.

YEARNING FOR THE SIMPLE LIFE

It is also about that time that the name 'Anne Hathaway's Cottage' was first coined. Interest in viewing Shakespeare-related places had been growing since the late eighteenth century, and visitors wanted to see the place where Shakespeare's wife was born and raised. (Such trips were made easier when the railway came to Stratford-upon-Avon in 1864.) Over the course of the next fifty years, the farm gradually became a garden.[1] By 1850, the barn had been pulled down and, by the 1860s, there were shrubs near the house; to the south were vegetable-growing areas that looked rather like allotments, with cabbages, currants and climbing beans. Photographs from the late nineteenth century show that the house had been 'prettified' with a few roses, rosemary bushes and hollyhocks (*Alcea*) and the exterior of the house itself began to take on a more 'cared-for' appearance.

The nineteenth century saw a rise in the interest in cottages and the 'simple' life, fuelled by the interest in poets such as Dorothy and William Wordsworth living out a rural idyll at Dove Cottage in the Lake District, and by the writings of Mary Russell Mitford, who described the pretty cottage gardens of Hampshire.[2] This was a time when romance met reality, when smallholders were creating gardens that not only supplied a family with their vegetables and soft fruit, but also had room for sweet peas (*Lathyrus odoratus*), aubretia, phlox, delphiniums, campanulas, lupins, peonies and sweet Williams (*Dianthus barbatus*) as well as ornamental shrubs, such as rock roses (*Cistus*), heathers (*Erica* and *Calluna*) and fuchsias. These were gardens to show off to the neighbours and in which to grow produce that would win prizes at village shows. It was also the period in which 'florists' flowers', which had achieved extraordinary popularity a century earlier, were still cultivated by working people – 'improved' cottage flowers such as carnations (*Dianthus*), polyanthus and auriculas (both types of *Primula*) and tulips.

Recognizing the growth in interest in Shakespeare tourism, and also in cottages and their gardens, the SBT bought Anne Hathaway's Cottage in 1892 from Thomas Barnes's estate for £3,000. One of the tenants of the three cottages was a widow, Mrs Baker, who had lived there for forty years, and she had already been showing visitors round on an ad hoc basis. The SBT asked her to stay on as custodian, which she did until her death in 1899. The cottage became a destination for painters, poets and writers as well as those inspired by the life of Shakespeare himself. Anne Hathaway's Cottage thus began to take on a wider cultural status than simply the childhood home of the wife of a sixteenth-century poet.

By the early twentieth century, Anne Hathaway's Cottage was starting to have a pretty garden, as depicted by William Wells Quatremain in 1900. Quatremain was well-known for his watercolours of Shakespeare's homes.

Primroses, Cowslips and Oxlips

And in the wood where often you and I
Upon faint primrose beds were wont to lie,
A Midsummer Night's Dream, Act 1 scene 1

When Shakespeare needs to conjure up images of spring and a rural setting, he often turns to *Primula* – primroses (*P. vulgaris*), oxlips (*P. elatior*) and cowslips (*P. veris*) – and it is clear he knows this flower group intimately. In gardens of the time, *Primula* of all types were widely grown, within knot gardens and in more simple garden settings. They were essentially wild flowers, collected and transplanted to gardens and then increased by division. In the sixteenth century, the wrinkled and coloured forms, which would morph into the decorative auriculas and coloured polyanthus of later centuries, were still a rarity known as 'collectors' flowers'.

Primulas appeared everywhere – on fabrics and textiles, in paintings and even on stained glass windows. Perdita in *The Winter's Tale* recognizes the difference between 'pale' primroses and 'bold oxlips'. The 'faintness' of primroses might be true – Gerard refers to *P. vulgaris* as being 'whitish yellow'. We would not call oxlips particularly 'bold' so Gerard may have been referring to the fact that it is tall – or to one of the naturally occurring crosses, which is now called false oxlip.

Cowslips are picked out for special attention in *Henry V*, where they are described as 'freckled' – a good description of the darker orange markings inside the flower of a cowslip.

Of the three primulas described above, cowslip is the most scented. It is also the food plant for the Duke of Burgundy fritillary butterfly. In *Henry V*, it is Burgundy who gives the speech about the decline of the French country:

That even mead – that erst brought sweetly forth
The freckled cowslip, burnet, and green clover –
Wanting the scythe, all uncorrected, rank,
Henry V, Act 5 scene 2

As often happens, it is Shakespeare creating language and future generations picking up his references to the natural world. His powers of observation are highly tuned – close scrutiny of a cowslip reveals that it would be just a perfect size for a sprite such as Ariel in *The Tempest*: 'In a cowslip's bell I lie.'[3]

Around Stratford-upon-Avon, primulas would have been widespread – in coppiced woodland, on banks, along hedgerows and in damp pastures. Cowslips in Warwickshire were known as 'cowslups', because they were found where cattle grazed – not quite as pretty an image as Ariel, but real nonetheless.

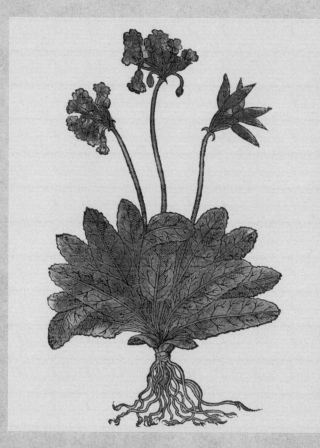

ABOVE Oxlips from John Gerard's *Herball* of 1597
OPPOSITE Primroses (*Primula vulgaris*) and cowslips (*P. veris*)

The renowned plantswoman Ellen Willmott designed the three large herbaceous borders in front of the house, in the 1920s.

MISS WILLMOTT'S GARDEN

In 1911, the minutes of an SBT committee meeting reveal that the garden was in a poor condition. The wife of a committee member, the Hon. Mrs Hodson, offered and was duly dispatched to oversee improvement works which included laying out new stone and gravel paths. But the garden's real revival came in the 1920s, when the need to lay a new sewer across the garden precipitated a chance to do new works, and it was decided to invite Miss Ellen Willmott to advise.

Willmott, who gives her name to many plants including Miss Willmott's ghost (*Eryngium giganteum*), was a celebrated plantswoman and designer of the time. Brought up at Warley Place in Essex, she was one of two women awarded the RHS Victoria medal of honour in 1897 – the other being Gertrude Jekyll.

At a meeting of 9 December 1923: 'Miss Willmott explained her suggestions for relaying & replanting the garden there, and after a lengthy discussion, it was proposed . . . that the sum of not exceeding £25 be spent on the necessary

trees & plants and the work on the paths & steps . . .'[14] She had already worked with Ernest Law on Shakespeare's garden at New Place (see page 170) and wasted no time before getting on with the revamp of Anne Hathaway's Cottage garden. By the end of January 1924, the work was complete except for the planting. Willmott had already spent £10 of her allotted budget, and a hundred gentian plants had been ordered. The budget was helped somewhat by a gift of twenty-five peony roots from a New York donor. In the summer of that year, Willmott turned her attention to the orchard, suggesting it would be improved by having a winding path through it; a year later, the trees were underplanted with 4,000 bulbs.

The garden was enclosed on the roadside by cleft oak palings and entered by an oak gate. Willmott designed the raised terrace and curved steps as well as the three herbaceous borders for which she left planting plans – these were to be filled with old-fashioned herbaceous plants, roses and simple topiary. Climbing roses were planted against the house. She added further borders, planting low box mounds in the corners and filling them with shrubs.

OPPOSITE Roses planted against the house include vibrant red *Rosa* 'Danse du Feu'.
ABOVE Giant mullein (*Verbascum thapsus*) thrives in the cottage borders.

The Poet's Wild Flowers

> I know a bank where the wild thyme blows,
> Where oxlips and the nodding violet grows,
> *A Midsummer Night's Dream*, Act 2 scene 1

Set in a fantasy world, the bank where Titania is sleeping is one of the most famous passages used to illustrate Shakespeare's familiarity with wild plants. It includes wild thyme (*Thymus polytrichus* subsp. *britannicus*) – a now rare wild plant in Britain – as well as those that are still familiar.

Shakespeare was not the only Warwickshire poet to draw on the county's rich heritage of wild flowers. His contemporary Michael Drayton, who spent much of his time in the village of Clifford Chambers just south of Stratford-upon-Avon, also reflected the Elizabethan taste for floral imagery in his poems.[5] Drayton's *The Shepheards Garland* (1593) was modelled on Edmund Spenser's flower-filled *Shepheardes Calender* (1579).

DAISIES, CUCKOOS AND SMOCKS

Shakespeare's most playful and youthful reference to wild flowers is in the 'Spring' song from *Love's Labour's Lost,* written when he was in his late twenties:

> When daisies pied and violets blue,
> And lady-smocks all silver white
> And cuckoo-buds of yellow hue
> Do paint the meadows with delight,
> *Love's Labour's Lost*, Act 5 scene 2

The cuckoo buds are probably buttercups (*Ranunculus*) – the word buttercup did not come into usage until the eighteenth century – but could equally be a host of other 'cuckoo' flowers and mean anything that flowered when the cuckoo returned in April. Cuckoo flower or lady's smock (*Cardamine pratensis*) has white flowers, which would have covered the damp meadows in spring, looking like a white sheet or a petticoat. The flower takes its name from the common Tudor practice of putting out smocks and other washing to dry on hedges.

Shakespeare proves that daisies (*Bellis perennis*) are well known to him when he calls them 'pied' – just as he also understands that they have no scent in *The Two Noble Kinsmen*.[6] Daisies were commonplace, but very useful, wild flowers used medicinally. Gerard says they are the 'best for physick', that is, better than the double garden forms, and advises them pounded with unsalted butter as a poultice for joint pains and gout.

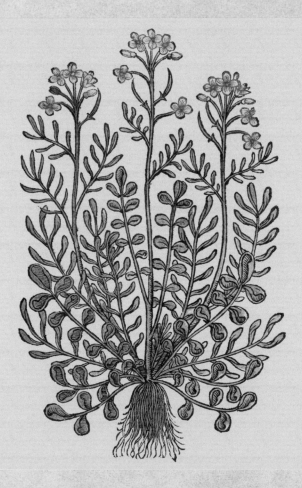

ABOVE Cuckoo flower or lady's smock (*Cardamine pratensis*)
OPPOSITE The traditionally managed meadow at Anne Hathaway's Cottage

The mainly apple and some pear trees, arranged in eight straight lines in the orchard, had been planted shortly before Willmott's interventions – the oldest ones are now ninety years old. In 1925, Willmott ordered an old tool shed in the north-western corner to be taken down and replaced with a thatched and timber building, built by the SBT's architect Guy Pemberton; this still stands just beyond what is now known as the Willmott Garden. The idea of having mown grass walks through the orchard, augmented by wild flowers and spring bulbs, is a legacy of Willmott that continues today and sits well with twenty-first-century garden taste.

DEVELOPMENT OF THE GARDEN

There is no evidence that Anne Hathaway and William Shakespeare ever lived at Shottery and they are more likely to have set up home with William's parents in Henley Street in Stratford. Nevertheless, various initiatives during the past twenty years have recognized the visitors' thirst for elements that link the garden more closely with the playwright himself. For example, in 1988, a former pasture was planted as the Shakespeare Tree Garden with forty trees directly referred to in Shakespeare's plays. The Tree Garden is also home to several sculptures, which were placed there in a joint initiative between the USA and the UK. Students from both countries were commissioned to make Shakespeare-inspired artworks, and chose a range of characters as their subject matter, including Hamlet, Brutus, King Lear, Falstaff and Titania. The sculptures create interest, particularly in winter, and they have become embedded in this part of the garden as the trees mature.

To mark Queen Elizabeth II's Silver Jubilee in 1977, a walk was instated to link woodland on the opposite side of the village lane with the cottage. In 1993, this was continued with the planting of 1,500 deciduous trees and shrubs beside the stream. Now known as the Shottery Brook Walk, this footpath winds along the waterside, with plantings of snowdrops (*Galanthus*) and aconites in winter, followed by snake's-head fritillaries (*Fritillaria meleagris*) and irises for spring and early summer. This is part of the SBT's mission to enhance the tranquillity of the site – and to allow visitors to find quiet spots even when Anne Hathaway's Cottage is at its busiest.

The vegetable plot at the western end of the house was added in the late 1990s as a way of making more of a link with the house's past and the food they would need to produce. A maze based on a sixteenth-century design by Thomas Hill was installed in 2001 involving the planting of 1,000 yews (*Taxus*). Despite extensive drainage, the yews have struggled, and it was eventually decided to take them out – leaving just an outer ring of, now mature, hedging.

'One touch of nature makes the whole world kin'

Troilus and Cressida,
Act 3 scene 3

History Play by Jane Lawrence is one of several artworks and sculptures picking up literary themes in the Shakespeare Tree Garden.

Snake's-head Fritillaries

And in his blood that on the ground lay spilled
A purple flower sprung up, chequered with white,
Resembling well his pale cheeks, and the blood
Which in round drops upon their whiteness stood.
Venus and Adonis

There is a question mark over the identify of the flower that springs up where the boy, Adonis, lies dead, in the poem *Venus and Adonis*. Shakespeare is generally exact when talking about flowers that he knows well, so the first line would seem to refer to snake's-head fritillary (*Fritillaria meleagris*), which grows in damp meadows. These have been planted along the brook next to Anne Hathaway's Cottage as a homage to the poet. However, Shakespeare goes on to say that the flowers are 'sweet smelling' which snake's-head fritillary is not, particularly.

Other candidates that have been put forward are wood anemones (*Anemone nemorosa*), but the chequered reference seems quite clear. Artistic licence might have overlooked the scent. However, no sixteenth- or seventeenth-century writers mention fritillaries as wild plants, and the writer Geoffrey Grigson concludes that they existed only in Tudor or Jacobean gardens (where Shakespeare could well have seen them) and from gardens they might have spread into the wild. Gerard refers to fritillaries as 'chequered daffodils'. Intriguingly, snake's-head fritillary seems to have had a long association with blood and death – it is, in fact, poisonous – and some of the other local English names associated with it include weeping widow and dead men's bells.

LEFT AND OPPOSITE Snake's-head fritillary (*Fritillaria meleagris*) growing beside Shottery Brook

THE GARDEN TODAY

Visitors today enter the 5 hectare/12 acre garden through a walkway of sweet peas (*Lathyrus odoratus*), trained up a framework of hazel twigs, cut from the garden. These heritage varieties change each year but always include the ones that arrived in Britain in the seventeenth century ('Cupani' and 'Matucana') and those with Shakespearian connections (such as white-flowered 'Romeo' and 'Juliet'). There is also salmon-pink 'Miss Willmott', named in 1906 for Ellen Willmott, the gardener who laid out gardens around the house.

The three cottage beds devised by Ellen Willmott are still very much as they have always been. Plants are divided and redistributed, but many are the original varieties that she introduced, including columbine (*Aquilegia*), lungwort (*Pulmonaria*), delphinium, cranesbill (*Geranium*), gentian, stachys, leucanthemum, oriental poppies (*Papaver orientale*) and primula. The style is relaxed, but, as with all large herbaceous borders, the gardeners at Anne Hathaway's Cottage are always managing the growth, making sure that one species or cultivar does not threaten to spoil the cottage-style mixed planting.

BELOW Sweet peas (*Lathyrus odoratus*) are trained up a framework of hazel twigs along the path leading to the cottage gardens.

OPPOSITE Roses and delphiniums line the path to the raised brick terrace designed by Ellen Willmott.

OVERLEAF A multi-stemmed mock orange (*Philadelpus coronarius*) stands in front of Anne Hathaway's Cottage. The large white rose to the left is *Rosa* 'Rambling Rector'.

Beyond the flower gardens, a willow arch leads into the oak plantation – an area of woodland which provides a useful shelter belt for the garden. Originally, the woodland was planted with 'nurse' trees (here, pines) that help the trunks of the oaks to grow upwards and dead straight. The pines have now done their job, and fifty of them will be taken out over the next few years, allowing the garden team to augment the woodland understorey with shade-loving shrubs and put in a full range of woodland plants. Bluebell (*Hyacinthoides non-scripta*) colonies have already been established and are increasing.

A recurring feature at Anne Hathaway's Cottage is the willow (*Salix*) – or osier – work, to be seen in screens, fences, tunnels, arbours and the crescent-moon sculpture by Tom Hare. The gardening team spend approximately 200 hours each year renewing the willow work in the garden. Osiers are cropped from the SBT's own willow (*Salix viminalis*) beds each year to provide material for the arbours and screens. These structures are maintained and renewed three times a year. When the stems first come into leaf in spring, the arbours and fences are inspected for any parts that have not greened up and might be dead. If so, new stems are cut and woven in to fill in the gaps. Then in May or June, any unruly growth is trimmed back to make sure visitors can still get inside the tunnels and arbours. In February, when the stems are dormant, the main weaving is done, firmly planting the willow wands in the earth, to fill out the structures.

Close to the cottage, the two vegetable beds are resown and planted every year with a variety of interesting salad and vegetable varieties including lovage (*Levisticum officinale*), corn salad (*Valerianella locusta*), lemon balm (*Melissa officinalis*) and good King Henry (*Chenopodium bonus-henricus*). 'Green Globe' artichokes are always a feature and a semi-permanent bed of blackcurrant 'Wellington' gives a good crop of fruit.

Beyond the cottage itself is the area known as the Dell, an area of old fruit trees and the thatched cabin suggested by Ellen Willmott. It has bulbs in early spring, but is usually kept closely mown. Beyond are two orchards managed under the Stewardship Scheme.[7] The first and older one is being controlled with a 'grazing' regime, whereby mowers cut the grass every three weeks to a height of 5 cm/2 inches to mimic the action of livestock. All the cuttings are taken away and composted, to prevent the build-up of high nutrients. In the second orchard, which is divided from the first orchard by an old ditch and hedge where primroses and cowslips grow in the spring, the grass is allowed to grow longer, before it is scythed down in July and cleared away – the traditional management routine of a hay meadow. In the autumn, the fruit is gathered by a local, not-for-profit initiative, and the fruits are given away to local school groups.[8] The orchards include plums, apples, medlar and pear

'Make me a willow cabin at your gate'

Twelfth Night, Act 1 scene 5

OPPOSITE Examples of hazel and willow work in the garden of Anne Hathaway's Cottage include (centre) sculptor Tom Hare's woven-willow crescent moon.

LEFT Areas devoted to medicinal and edible herbs have been created close to the house for growing chives, thyme, lovage (*Levisticum officinale*), sage (*Salvia officinalis*) and lemon balm (*Melissa officinalis*).

TOP Old-fashioned pea varieties are trained up hazel supports.

ABOVE Rows of vegetables make best use of the sunny slope.

Orchards

Nay, you shall see my orchard, where, in an arbour,
we will eat a last year's pippin of my own grafting,
with a dish of caraways, and so forth

There's a dish of leather-coats for you
Henry IV Part II, Act 5 scene 3

In Elizabethan England, a landholder of almost any size had an orchard or at the least a couple of fruit trees. There was an orchard attached to Shakespeare's birthplace in Henley Street when his father bought it, and there was a larger orchard attached to New Place, Shakespeare's last house. Both the Ardens and the Hathaways had substantial orchards.

As a setting for a scene within a play, the orchard had much to recommend it. It was a place where a gentleman could sit in an arbour or read a book: for example, in *Much Ado About Nothing*, Benedick asks for his book to be bought to the orchard, where he will spend time reading.[9] Hamlet's father's ghost claims he was murdered while taking his customary afternoon sleep in his orchard, and in *Henry IV Part II* (quoted above) Falstaff and company retire to Justice Shallow's orchard after dinner, where Shallow is proud to be able to offer apples which he has grafted and grown himself.

Shakespeare shows that he was familiar with the work going on in orchards. Grafting in particular is a skill that has changed little down the centuries – the process whereby a piece of wood with buds from a new variety (the scion) is grown on to a rootstock, usually a young whip of a strong-growing crab (*Malus*) or other apple. All that was needed to grow these new varieties was a sharp grafting knife and some kind of hessian or cloth binding to hold the graft in place.

CULTIVATED APPLES

No one threw as much money at acquiring all the finest varieties of apples as Henry VIII. At that time, a good orchard sapling cost six pence, compared with a penny for other deciduous trees. The king employed a 'fruitier' called Richard Harris, and amassed a large collection of fruit varieties from the continent at his orchard at Teynham in Kent, which covered 42.5 hectares/105 acres. Other gentlemen followed suit and took the chance to grow pears, medlars and pippins from Normandy. The last were one of the first cultivated apples, and pippin became a general term for late-fruiting, keeping apples or 'keepers', which suited the British climate. In 1611, John Tradescant travelled to Delft in Holland to buy apples, cherry, quince, medlars and pears for Robert Cecil. By the time of Parkinson's *Paradisi in Sole Paradisus Terrestris* of 1629, sixty varieties are recommended for growing including pearmains, codlings and costards. Shakespeare gives the name 'Costard' to a comic character in *Love's Labour's Lost*. Codling became the name of a later apple variety, but to Shakespeare it meant a young unripe apple.

Shakespeare mentions caraways and leather-coats in the Justice Shallow scene (quoted above). Caraway is an old Cotswold apple no longer grown and leather-coat may be the russet apple still cultivated today. Alternatively, Shakespeare may actually have been referring to caraway seeds, which were a fashionable accompaniment to apples at the end of a meal.

PEARS AND MEDLARS

The medlar (*Mespilus germanica*) appears in *As You Like It* when Rosalind refers to it being rotten before it is half-ripe – 'that's the right virtue of the medlar'. This is a reference to the tradition of 'bletting' a medlar, that is waiting until it is rotten before eating it.[10]

Two varieties of pear get a mention in Shakespeare's plays. In *Romeo and Juliet* a 'Poperin' was possibly a pear named after the town of Poperinge, which is near Ypres in the Low Countries. More likely, it was a name chosen for the suggestive way it sounded – linking

Romeo's 'pear' with Juliet's 'medlar' – both fruits having sexual connotations.

In *The Winter's Tale*, the shepherd is sent to get saffron for the 'warden pie' – warden pears being red cooking pears. At the time, fruit was generally eaten cooked, as the Elizabethans were suspicious of raw fruit and the advice was always to bake or roast pears. The warden was grown by monks in the fourteenth century and originates from the village of Old Warden in Bedfordshire. It is a firm pear that does not disintegrate on cooking; it also keeps well from late autumn right through the winter.

CRAB APPLES

Crab apples (*Malus*) were fruits of the hedgerow and woodland – the tart taste being in stark contrast to the sweeter cultivated apples of the orchard. 'Crab' seems to have been used to mean sour – the crab being the last one to be picked, in love as well as in gardening. It is included in this way in *The Taming of the Shrew*, when Petruchio says: 'Why here's no crab; and therefore look not sour.'[11] Crab apples were roasted, to soften them, and the song at the end of *Love's Labour's Lost* conjures up a winter scene with a teaming bowl of hot wine, flavoured with cloves, the apples bobbing up and down:

When roasted crabs hiss in the bowl,
Then nightly sings the staring owl:
Love's Labour's Lost, Act 5 scene 2

'Worcester' apples (*Malus*)

Medlars (*Mespilus germanica*)

Crab apples (*Malus*)

trees and a healthy crop of mistletoe (*Viscum album*). Pruning there is carried out from December to March, when any dead limbs are removed from the trees to ensure they are as productive as possible. Some of the orchard trees are approaching a century of growth while many of the more recently planted ones are just coming into full fruit production. This mix of ages ensures that the orchard will be sustainable into the future.

TOGETHER FOREVER?

The marriage of Anne Hathaway and William Shakespeare forever linked this small hamlet with the playwright. Yet, Anne and William spent much of their married life apart – something that has often left Anne portrayed as the 'forgotten' wife. There are no records of Anne's life between the baptism of her twins (Judith and Hamnet), in 1585, until her death in 1623, when she is buried beside William in Holy Trinity Church. There is no reason, however, to believe that their marriage did not endure while William lived away from Stratford-upon-Avon. When his financial situation improved, William bought a house and garden not in London but in Stratford-upon-Avon, a family home, and probably for the first time he and Anne were independent of their parents.

Since being planted at the beginning of the twentieth century, plums, pears, medlars, quince and cherry trees have been added to the original orchard.

The Garden Visitor

Shakespeare in London

My lord of Ely, when I was last in Holborn
I saw good strawberries in your garden there.
I do beseech you send for some of them.

Richard III, Act 3 scene 4

William Shakespeare spent a substantial part of his life
away from his home town. As an actor, playwright and
theatre shareholder, his working world was in the capital
city. We know he was in London by 1592 and he carried
on this dual existence between Stratford-upon-Avon and
London throughout the 1590s and 1600s. This gave him the
opportunity to see other interesting houses and gardens
belonging to members of the court, professional colleagues,
and friends with more modest incomes.

A pair of old mulberry (*Morus nigra*) trees can be seen in the fountain court
of Middle Temple, one of London's four ancient Inns of Court.

THE INNS OF COURT GARDENS

THERE IS A THEORY THAT Shakespeare may have first gone to London on behalf of his father, in the late summer of 1588, in connection with the court case they were fighting to win back Mary Arden's land.[1] The idea that Shakespeare's first introduction to London might have been through the law courts is attractive to anyone interested in gardens and early theatre.

The first documented mention of a performance of a Shakespeare play was at Gray's Inn, one of the four Inns of Court, on 28 December 1594. It was *The Comedy of Errors* and it took place as part of the Christmas festivities. Law students lived in the courts and were very involved in performing, staging and watching theatre and were one of the key audiences that Elizabethan playwrights wrote for. Shakespeare certainly has a firm grasp of the nuances of law and, if his first taste of London was through the Inns, he would have seen some of the best gardens in London.

BELOW This sixteenth-century plan of London shows Fleet Street, Temple Bar and the Temple Garden running down to the River Thames.

OPPOSITE The Shakespeare Birthplace Trust portrait, formerly known as the Ellenborough portrait, was painted between 1610 and 1615. It is one of several early copies of the Cobbe portrait (see page 13).

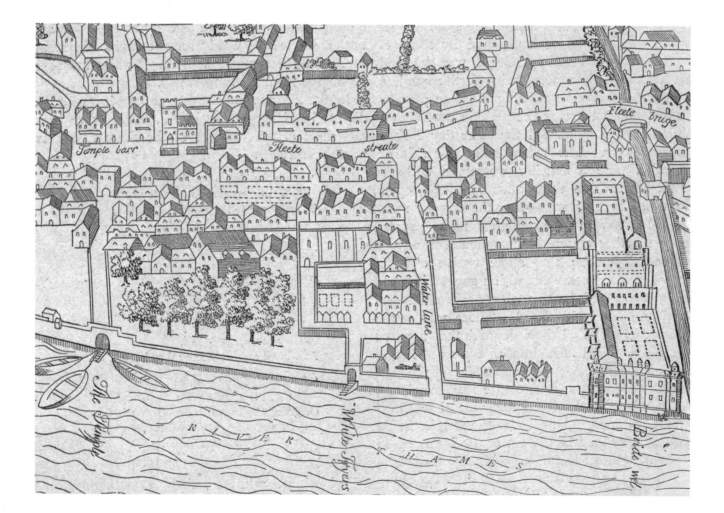

ABOVE The woodland garden of the Inner Temple forms part of the Temple Garden – a place that Shakespeare would have known.

OPPOSITE The peony garden (here with its spring planting) is part of the 1.25 hectare/3 acre-gardens of the Inner Temple. Parts of the site date to the fourteenth century.

The four Inns of Courts – Gray's Inn, Lincoln's Inn, Inner Temple and Middle Temple – all had gardens and these remain some of the oldest green spaces in London. The Temple Garden beside the Thames is where Shakespeare decided to set the famous, red-and-white-roses scene in *Henry VI Part I*.[2] In Shakespeare's time there was an orchard there, and a more formal design, with a top terrace and walks, was laid out in 1591. This 1.25-hectare/3-acre garden still acknowledges its long associations with Shakespeare and includes walnuts (*Juglans regia*), a medlar (*Mespilus germanica*), quince (*Cydonia oblonga*) and black mulberry (*Morus nigra*). Many of the sixteenth-century buildings of the Inner Temple were destroyed in the Great Fire of London of 1666 but the garden remains, and is from at least the fourteenth century.

Gray's Inn gardens – known as The Walks – were laid out in 1606 by Sir Francis Bacon (then Treasurer of the Inn). Bacon had a summer house built on a mount, and there were flower gardens – perhaps with Bacon's recommended

plants: the double white violet, wallflowers (*Erysimum*), gillyflowers (*Dianthus caryophyllus*), cowslips (*Primula veris*), irises and lilies. Bacon would have seen performances of Shakespeare's plays and was most likely echoing those when he wrote his famous essay *Of Gardens* in 1625. The flower gardens at Gray's Inn were later replaced with avenues of clipped trees and have become one of London's treasured open spaces – the ancient Indian bean tree (*Catalpa*), which is reputed to have been planted by Bacon, probably arrived a century later.

A number of smaller Inns of Chancery, such as Clement's Inn and Clifford's Inn, were the training establishments for young lawyers. In *Henry IV Part II*, Justice Shallow looks back fondly to his wild days at Clement's Inn.[3] Staple Inn was used by wool merchants as a place to stay and carry out transactions – another possible connection with John and William Shakespeare. The gardens of these smaller Inns have not survived, but they would have also held theatrical productions in their gardens and halls.

'You had not four such swinge-bucklers in all the Inns o' Court again'

Henry IV Part II, Act 3 scene 2

'Since I have hemmed
thee here
Within the circuit of
this ivory pale'

Venus and Adonis

Shakespeare's first works were
dedicated to Henry Wriothesley,
the third Earl of Southampton. The
earl was imprisoned in the Tower of
London from 1601 to 1603, for his
involvement in the Essex rebellion
against Elizabeth I.

THE PLAGUE YEAR

Shakespeare was certainly known in London by 1592, and probably lived in
Bishopsgate. This was close to the famous Bucklersbury market mentioned by
Falstaff in *The Merry Wives of Windsor*, when he describes young men who 'smell
like Bucklersbury in simple time'.[4] Two streets that come off Bishopsgate give a
clue as to the area's importance as a source of herbs and other medicinal plants;
these are Wormwood Street and Camomile Street. It was at this time that
Shakespeare appeared in print for the first time, when, in April 1593, his poem
Venus and Adonis was published; it was dedicated to the Earl of Southampton,
Henry Wriothesley.

However, just as Shakespeare's career was beginning to take off, the plague
struck. In January 1593, the Privy Council had banned all social gatherings

where plague could spread – and that included playhouses. It is likely that Shakespeare spent part of 'the plague year' staying at Southampton's house, the former Titchfield Abbey in Hampshire (which became 'Place House' when the monasteries were dissolved under Henry VIII). Southampton's ancestor, Thomas Wriothesley, had converted the abbey to a house by knocking through the nave of the old church and turning the cloister into an inner courtyard with a fountain. If Shakespeare did stay there, he would have seen new gardens as well as the linear medieval fish ponds and extensive deer park. Shakespeare would also have been aware of the history of Titchfield Abbey: Margaret of Anjou married Henry VI there on 23 April 1445. Henry VI was the subject of Shakespeare's first series of history plays, written in the early 1590s.

THE SOUTH BANK AND THE GLOBE

When the theatres reopened in 1594, Richard Burbage was key in forming the Lord Chamberlain's Men. Shakespeare was part of this new company, and when they needed a permanent home it was decided to use the timbers from the old Shoreditch Theatre to make a new one on the south bank. In 1599, to raise money for the new theatre, they issued shares – half to Burbage

The South Bank of the River Thames in 1572, before the building of the Globe Theatre, was still open fields and gardens.

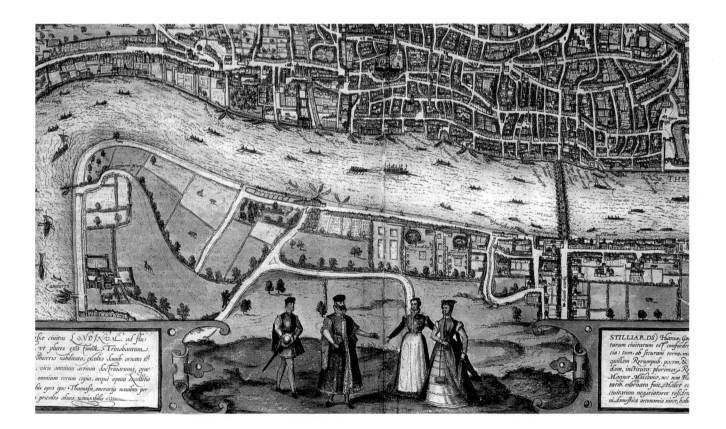

The Globe Theatre (here on the right) was built by the Lord Chamberlain's Men, in 1599. It burnt down during a performance of *Henry VIII* in 1613, after which it was quickly rebuilt.

and the remainder divided equally between a number of the actors, including Shakespeare, John Heminges (who would later initiate the First Folio), Thomas Pope and Will Kempe.

The Globe itself was on the site of seven gardens, next to a park. It seems that the Lord Chamberlain's Men not only constructed the most amazing theatre – housing 1,500 people and having a motto that loosely translates as 'All the World's a Stage' – but they also built a new house with a garden next door for the acting company. A document dated 17 July 1599 states that this house and garden were 'in the occupation of William Shakespeare and others'. Shakespeare never set up home alone in London, but was always in lodgings, where he could presumably live more cheaply.[5] So we now get a glimpse of the thirty-five-year-old Shakespeare involved in renovating an old house and garden at his New Place in Stratford (bought in 1597), as well as overseeing a brand-new house and garden on the south bank of the Thames.

LONDON GARDENS OF THE 1590S

Shakespeare was in London during one of the most exciting periods in the city's history. Between 1580 and 1600, the population doubled to around 200,000 inhabitants. John Stow's survey of London between 1592 and 1603 indicates that there were lots of small town gardens, particularly outside the city walls and south of the Thames – gardens with orchards, fruit, vegetables and flowers. In this, Shakespeare's most prolific period of playwriting, he must have seen gardens belonging to all sectors of society from royal palaces to more modest artisan gardens. Yet, even London, which in 1598 had sixteen markets selling fresh produce daily sourced from the counties and speciality foods from overseas, felt the effects of the disastrous harvests of 1594–7. No wheat, rye or barley coming to town meant no bread, the staple food. Richard Gardiner, who wrote the first book specifically on growing vegetables, *Profitable Instructions for the Manuring, Sowing and Planting of Kitchin Gardens* (1599), was so worried by the starvation that he produced

Thomas Hill – a Londoner writing in the mid-sixteenth century – aimed his gardening advice at the owners of town houses. In this image from *The Gardeners Labyrinth*, gardeners are making a shady walk, using cut lengths of willow (*Salix*) or hazel (*Corylus*) and climbing plants.

In *The Gardeners Labyrinth*, Hill depicts plots that were enclosed by fences or hedges, with wooden ballustrades, simple knots, generous paths and clipped hedges, giving us a good idea of what a London garden might have looked like in the late sixteenth century.

700 cabbages from his own 1.6 hectare/4 acre garden to feed the poor. His book encouraged people to grow carrots and other root vegetables. Even those who had no land, he believed, could grow these root vegetables on dung heaps, which were plentiful outside the city walls.

GARDENS FOR PLEASURE AND PHYSIC

He hath a garden circummured with brick,
Whose western side is with a vineyard backed;
And to that vineyard is a planked gate,
That makes his opening with this bigger key.
This other doth command a little door
Which from the vineyard to the garden leads.
There have I made my promise
Upon the heavy middle of the night
To call upon him.
Measure for Measure, Act 4 scene 1

'Our bodies are
our gardens, to the
which our wills are
gardeners'

Othello, Act 1 scene 3

Holland's Leaguer, a notorious
brothel in Southwark, here shown in
a seventeenth-century woodcut, had
a garden enclosed by a moat, with
an arbour seat, fruit tree and neat
rectangular beds.

Gardens for pleasure were a feature of city life – somewhere for the well-heeled
to go bowling, watch entertainments or eat in small banqueting houses. There
was a close link between gardens and playhouses – the gardens being somewhere
to go after the plays were finished. Shakespeare gives us a very detailed picture
of the geography of a walled garden with its adjoining vineyard in *Measure for
Measure*. City gardens also became associated with more lurid uses – for trysts
and private parties – and had a reputation for sex and prostitution.

Shakespeare's lodgings in the early years of the seventeenth century
would have brought him closer still to the world of herbalists, physicians and
apothecaries. Between the years 1603 and 1605, Shakespeare rented rooms in
a house on Silver Street, within the north-west corner of the London city walls.
Just around the corner from Shakespeare's lodging house was the garden of
the Hall of Barber-Surgeons' Company on Muggle or Monkwell Street, and the
Agas map of 1560 shows clearly laid-out beds of, presumably, herbs and physic
plants of use to surgeons. John Gerard, who was an official of the Barber-
Surgeons' Company and became its master in 1607, advised on the layout

John Gerard's Herball

The most famous physician and plantsman of the sixteenth and seventeenth centuries was, without doubt, John Gerard. His was not the first herbal in English, but it was the first to give detailed instructions on the use of each plant as a cure, as well as a description of the plant and where it grows. As a member of the Company of Barber-Surgeons in London, as well as garden superintendent to William Cecil (Lord High Treasurer and Private Secretary to Elizabeth I) and so caring for Cecil's gardens on the Strand and at Theobalds in Essex, Gerard was well placed to observe, collect and study the nature of plants.

Gerard was born in Nantwich, Cheshire in 1545 but lived and worked in London for most of his life. He had his own garden in Fetter Lane, Holborn, which he called 'the little plot of myne own', and the plants he grew were published in his *Catalogue* of 1596 – the first complete plant list from a single garden ever printed. Far more extensive was *The Herball or Generall Historie of Plantes* – the first edition (1597) running to more than a thousand pages, with 1,800 woodblock prints. This was the culmination of Gerard's work and lists (probably) everything that had been imported into Britain at that time.

Gerard's garden in Holborn was not the first to feature interesting and unusual plants in London. In the 1540s, William Turner had worked at Syon House as the Duke of Somerset's private physician and had built up an early collection of 'physic' plants. However, full-scale botanic or 'physic' gardens did not yet exist: Oxford Botanic Garden was not founded until 1621, and was followed by Edinburgh Botanic Garden in 1670 and Chelsea Physic Garden in 1673.

Gerard's *Herball* was published in three parts: the first book covered reeds, grasses and bulbs; the second was on herbs 'for meat, medicine or sweet smelling use'; and the third described trees, roses, fruit-bearing plants and even mosses and mushrooms. It was encyclopaedic, although tending towards the cultivated rather than the wild forms of plants. If Shakespeare did read Gerard's work, it was probably to learn about those plants that had lately come into Britain such as crown imperials (*Fritillaria imperialis*), new species of flower-de-luce (*Iris*) and new fruits such as mulberries (*Morus*) and pomegranates (*Punica*).

For lively reading, Gerard is hard to beat: anyone wondering what to do with their onions in 1597 could learn that they should be 'stamped with salt, rue and honey, and so applied, they are good against the biting of a mad dog'.

Others would follow his lead – notably John Parkinson, who gives us the first fully worked-out encyclopaedia of plants available to gardeners in *Paradisi in Sole Paradisus Terrestris* (1629).

John Gerard, author of *The Herball or Generall Historie of Plantes*

of the garden. The company records state that it was planted with a hedge of eglantine roses (*Rosa rubiginosa*), vines, rosemary, violets and strawberries.

Whether or not Shakespeare actually met John Gerard or visited Gerard's garden in Holborn, it seems likely that he used or had his own reference copy of Gerard's *Herball or Generall Historie of Plantes*. He certainly cannot have been unaware of the growing trade in plants. Towards the end of the sixteenth century, huge quantities were arriving by ship to furnish the gardens of the rich. These would have been organized by merchants such as Nicholas Leate (active between 1590 and 1630), who traded with Turkey and Syria and employed collectors to bring in crown imperials (*Fritillaria imperialis*), Turk's cap lilies and anemones to furnish the new fashion for 'windflowers'. Crown imperials get a mention in only one of Shakespeare's later plays – *The Winter's Tale* – and probably did not arrive in Britain until after 1580. Through his continued residence in London, Shakespeare's experience of new plants was expanding and augmenting his innate knowledge of British native flowers.

MOVING ON

The 1590s were a time of uncertainty for the theatrical world. Shakespeare's output during this decade was fast and furious – at least two plays per year. Plague, however, was never far away, and the theatres were closed repeatedly – sometimes for a year or more at a time. In the summer of 1596, when the theatres were closed and the Lord Chamberlain's Men were touring the south of England, Shakespeare received news of his son Hamnet's death, aged eleven. Shakespeare might have thought it was time to return to his family. A year later, he would buy his first property in Stratford-upon-Avon. His artistic and working life was in London, but when he decided to buy land, houses and gardens it would be in his home town – the subject of the next two chapters.

Crown imperials as depicted in Gerard's *Herball* were among the new plants available to gardeners.

In Sickness and in Health
Hall's Croft

Within the infant rind of this weak flower
Poison has residence, and medicine power,

Romeo and Juliet, Act 2 scene 2

Hall's Croft begins to play its part in the story when Shakespeare
was at the height of his fame with some of his greatest plays
written and in circulation. In 1602 and still under forty years old,
Shakespeare bought 43.3 hectares/107 acres of land in Old Stratford
– an area just outside the jurisdiction of the 'new' borough (itself
founded in the late twelfth century). He paid £320 for a parcel that
included orchards, pasture and open field arable land. This was
the land that he would give to his twenty-four-year-old daughter
Susanna on her marriage to John Hall in 1607, on which they would
build their own house – now known as Hall's Croft.

Hall's Croft was built for Shakespeare's daughter Susanna and her husband, doctor John Hall.
The house dates from 1613, at which time the garden would have included many of the plants Hall used in his practice.

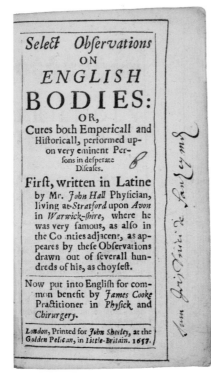

ON THEIR WEDDING, the couple inherited the land in Old Stratford and, with these rents and the steady success of Hall's medical practice, they were very comfortably off. In 1613, it is believed they built a timber-framed house we now know as Hall's Croft, right on the boundary of the old and new boroughs of Stratford – the boundary is still visible running through the middle of the garden.

The house itself was not known about until the nineteenth century, and there are other candidates for where the Halls could have lived.[1] However, it was a short walk from Shakespeare's own house at New Place (see page 157); the couple probably lived at New Place with Anne and Susanna's sister Judith (who had just turned twenty-two) until their own house was built.

John Hall was a devout man, serving as churchwarden at nearby Holy Trinity – the Shakespeares' family church. He was the son of a Bedfordshire doctor and had probably travelled abroad – possibly studying at the earliest botanic garden in Europe at Montpellier, founded in 1593, where he would have acquired an encyclopaedic and practical knowledge of plants. Shakespeare and John Hall became close – John was only eleven years his junior – and they acted together in property negotiations and other business dealings. *Pericles, Prince of Tyre* was written in the year that Susanna married John Hall and includes the clever doctor Cerimon, who revives the apparently dead Thaisa.[2] In *Cymbeline*, written three years later, it is the court physician Cornelius who reveals that the poison taken by the queen was not fatal after all.[3]

DOCTOR HALL'S CASEBOOK

We are fortunate that Susanna's husband made records of many of the patients he treated. *Select Observations*, which was translated from the Latin and published after his death in 1657, details the treatments that he administered and to whom.[4]

By the end of the sixteenth century, a three-tier medical system had developed: the physician, the surgeon (which included the elite barber-surgeons) and the apothecary. Surgeons and apothecaries were numerous – a town such as Stratford-upon-Avon might have several surgeons and apothecaries – but not every town had a physician. He was essentially a consultant who would have to travel to see his patients. From Hall's casebook, we know that he travelled within a 64 kilometre/40 mile radius of Stratford-upon-Avon to visit men and women (but predominantly women) of different faiths and ages – the oldest living until ninety-three. The range of ailments included falling sickness (epilepsy), gout, wind, consumption and syphilis, for which he would have prescribed (mainly) plant-based remedies and charged accordingly.

ABOVE Shakespeare's son-in-law, John Hall, kept detailed notes in Latin about his medical practice. They were printed in English for the first time in 1657 and record the herbs and other ingredients in use at the time.

OPPOSITE *Magnolia grandiflora* and a *Wisteria sinensis* are planted against the timber-framed house.

TOP AND ABOVE Drugs were stored in ceramic jars – these two Italian examples belong to the Shakespeare Birthplace Trust. The one with the spout was used for 'wet' potions, the other for 'dry' powders.

MEDICINE FOR THE BODY AND SOUL

When Hall was practising in the early seventeenth century, a physician could refer to a range of Latin and Greek texts, which gave the classical remedies, and there were also invaluable English herbals by William Turner (1551–68), William Bullein (1562–3) and John Gerard (1597).

The belief was that any ill health was caused by an imbalance of the four humours (choler, phlegm, melancholy and blood), which each had a corresponding colour (yellow, green, black and red). A physician would have asked a lot of questions about the patient's mental and physical state to assess the state of these humours. Examination was mainly external, but assessment would be made of the urine. The physician would then administer the drug that opposed the humours: for a cold moist illness such as phlegm, for example, hot dry remedies would be given. Every plant was either hot or cold; summer herbs such as lavender and mint (*Mentha*), for example, were hot. Foods also took on these properties: lettuce, for example, was cold and moist and could therefore help with hot dry fevers.

Hall would have practised occasional bloodletting, but his main treatments were purges (using rhubarb or imported senna) and emetics, to induce vomiting. Each preparation contained a large number of different ingredients, hence the high cost. In his case notes for Sir Nicholas Fortescue of Worcestershire, aged thirty-eight (a Catholic and a great drinker, apparently), Hall records using: liquorice, roots of succory (*Cichorium intybus*, which is also known as chicory), watercress, fumitory, centaury (*Centaurium*), rhubarb, flowers of chamomile, elder buds, seeds of fennel and saffron in one remedy.

The ingredients that made up the ointments, syrups, pills and powders were stored in ceramic jars, labelled in Latin. Examples of these can be seen in Hall's consulting room at the back of Hall's Croft today. They included powdered gemstones and precious metals, such as silver and gold, and some exceedingly dangerous metals, such as mercury (which was widely used as a treatment for syphilis).

HERBS AND SIMPLES

Single herbs – the raw ingredients – were known as 'simples' and were collected by herb gatherers who would sell them to apothecaries to make into 'compounds' for more elaborate medicines. The verb 'to simple' meant to go and collect herbs. Most 'simples' were bought from apothecaries – there were several in Stratford – or could be ordered from London. Peony root or black hellebore (*Helleborus niger*), which was used to treat melancholy, could not have been grown in sufficient quantities in the garden and would

Saffron

The term 'saffron' was used interchangeably to mean 'crocus' – saffron coming from the Arabic word for crocus. According to the early herbal of William Turner (1551), saffron was known as a plant remedy: 'The root drunken in sack maketh a man water well' – sack being the fortified, sherry-like wine that was popular in Elizabethan taverns and homes and was most famously drunk to excess by Shakespeare's character Falstaff.

Saffron – the delicate filaments harvested from the centre of the autumn-flowering crocus (*Crocus sativus*) – had been grown as a crop in Britain (particularly around the town of Saffron Walden in Essex) since the fourteenth century. Turner claims that apothecaries use 'bastard saffron' (*Colchicum autumnale*), the bulb of which if eaten is poisonous and the stigmas do not have the flavour or the full colour of the 'real' saffron.

Both types were used to starch ruffs and collars and as a colouring in cakes and baking. The crocuses were planted in summer then harvested in late autumn. Each flower had to be hand-picked and then carefully pulled apart to remove the red stigmas. The harvest was back-breaking work as it took some 4,000 flowers to yield just 28g (1oz) of the spice.

Saffron gets several mentions in Shakespeare's plays. Sometimes, this is to indicate colour – the rich yellow/orange colour of the strands – while elsewhere it is introduced as a real 'spice', which would have been available in markets, particularly in London. In *The Winter's Tale*, the clown believes that the sheep shearing feast will not complete without 'saffron, to colour the warden pies'.[5] The saffron is here used in the pastry to give it a stronger and more appetizing colour.

Herbalist John Gerard includes it in a complicated drink for those who are infected with 'pestilence' or plague. The remedy includes (ten strands of) saffron, mead, figs and ground walnuts; it probably would have tasted pleasant, if nothing else. Gerard states that saffron crocus is good (in moderation) for the heart, lungs and head. It was all about getting the dose right – too much would prevent sleep while the right amount would liven up the senses. This suggests that saffron crocus was quite a powerful and expensive ingredient and one that physicians would have used carefully.

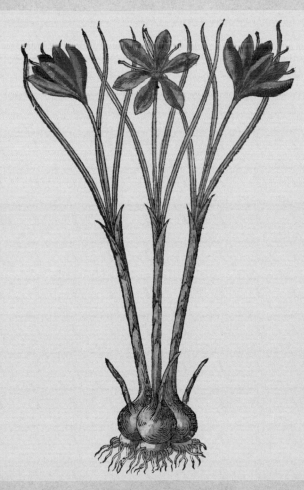

Saffron in flower from John Gerard's *Herball* of 1597

have been bought in as a powder. Expensive commodities such as saffron and cumin were common in medicine as well as for flavouring food. We know that Hall bought powders of aloewood, cinnamon, mace, nutmeg, cardamom and galangal. He may even have employed an on-site apothecary to work for him.

Common garden shrubs and herbs in frequent demand included English and French lavender (*Lavandula × intermedia* and *L. stoechas*), wormwood (*Artemisia absinthium*), rosemary, mints, juniper, hyssop, chicory (*Cichorium intybus*), lovage (*Levisticum officinale*), parsley (*Petroselinum crispum*), sorrel (*Rumex acetosa*), sage and radish (*Raphanus*) – all of which could be grown easily in the garden. Others had to be collected from the wild by herb collectors: for example, scabious, bugloss (*Echium vulgare*), fumitory (*Fumaria officinalis*), corn poppy (*Papaver rhoeas*), wood sorrel (*Oxalis acetosella*), betony (*Betonica officinalis*), docks (*Rumex obtusifolius*) and bistort (*Polygonum bistorta*).

One of the greatest threats to health in the sixteenth and early seventeenth century was plague, although most physicians had no idea how to combat it.

Doctors and apothecaries kept their receipts (prescriptions) in a lockable chest. This one was made of oak and holly between 1550 and 1625 and is lined with Elizabethan wallpaper.

One of the reputed cures included the root of gillyflowers or garden carnations (*Dianthus caryophyllus*; see panel page 140). This could partly account for why they were so widely grown in gardens throughout Shakespeare's lifetime. Other remedies involved aloes and apples, or cordials of rosemary, juniper, sorrel, cinnamon and saffron, which sound quite palatable. Perfumed tobacco was said to ward off plague, as was a mixture of treacle and gunpowder.

Roses were one of the mainstay ingredients of the potions. Hall's own notes list sixty uses of the plant in the form of rose water, ground powders, seeds, oils and distillations. He seems also to have prescribed watercress (*Nasturtium officinale*) and scurvy grass (*Cochlearia officinalis*) (which have high doses of ascorbic acid) to treat scurvy caused by a lack of fresh fruit and vegetables. However, if the potions were heated, which they often were, this would have destroyed the vitamin C. For the 'falling sickness' (epilepsy), Hall used peonies – the root hung around the neck and the hair powdered with the root, as well as rue and white wine vinegar sponged around the nostrils, which he claimed stopped the fits.

The importance of healthy eating was beginning to be recognized, and James I's physician, Theodore Mayern, suggested a daily intake for the king of chicory, sorrel, purslane, borage, thyme, vervain, dill, fennel and rocket. This advice would have trickled down slowly to other physicians and other gardens, perhaps even to the Halls, who would have wanted to stay abreast of current thinking.

THE SINISTER POWER OF PLANTS

Not poppy nor mandragora
Nor all the drowsy syrups of the world
Shall ever medicine thee to that sweet sleep
Which thou owedst yesterday.
Othello, Act 3 scene 3

Drugs are ever present in the plays of Shakespeare. *Othello*, *Macbeth* and *King Lear* were written in the years leading up to Susanna's marriage to John Hall, and Shakespeare could conceivably have talked to Hall about the use of potions. Even in the plays written much earlier, his interest in the power of plants is evident. In *Romeo and Juliet*, the friar is both the collector of the herbs and the practitioner.[6] In *A Midsummer Night's Dream*, Titania is 'doped' with the juice of a wild pansy. And Hamlet's father is poisoned by an unknown substance 'hebenon', which has been linked to yew (*Taxus*), hemlock (*Conium maculatum*) and henbane (*Hyoscyamus niger*). Herbalist William Turner said henbane 'make men mad, and fall into a great sleep'.

'Fetch me that flower; the herb I showed thee once'

A Midsummer Night's Dream, Act 2 scene 1

Pinks, Carnations and Gillyflowers

Sir, the year growing ancient,
Not yet on summer's death, nor on the birth
Of trembling winter, the fairest
flowers o'th' season
Are our carnations and streaked gillyvors,
The Winter's Tale, Act 4 scene 4

Dianthus were ubiquitous in Elizabethan and Jacobean gardens, being grown for both their medicinal and their aesthetic qualities. In the home, too, the branched shape and simple flowers were a popular motif on soft furnishings and plasterwork.

'Pink' is the oldest of the three common names for *Dianthus* but there is still much discussion as to which is the oldest – or the true – native species. A good candidate might be maiden pink (*D. deltoides*), which is scattered throughout Britain, or the common or wild pink (*D. plumarius*), which, despite its name, came from south-eastern Europe and has flourished there and in Britain depending on the prevailing climatic conditions, becoming naturalized only in the warmer southern parts of England.

Sweet William (*D. barbatus*) is said to have arrived from Normandy, in France, on imported building stone used to erect William the Conqueror's castles, though some writers put its first appearance at the much later date of 1573.

Carnation and gillyflower (from the Old French *gilofre*, *girofle* – in origin meaning clove, but in common usage meaning 'July flower') refer to *D. caryophyllus*, which is sometimes called clove stock or double clove carnation. Carnations and gillyflowers are thought to have moved north through Europe during the fifteenth century, reaching England in the sixteenth century. By the time John Gerard is writing his herbal, before 1597, they are so numerous and so infinite in variety that he says: 'every yeare every clymate and country bringeth forth new sorts'.

Often, gillyflower just seems to be a generic name given to all sorts of variations on the basic pink, including carnations and sweet Williams. All were grown for the scent, which was strong and rather like cloves.

Gerard talks of carnations being kept in pots because of the harsh winters, while gillyflowers were hardier and could go out in the garden. Carnation can be used as a description of colour too (as Shakespeare does in *Love's Labour's Lost* – the use of 'pink' as a colour was not current at this date). The flowers were also picked to make a perfumed conserve with sugar, which Gerard says doth 'wonderfully comfort the heart if taken now and then'.

Shakespeare clearly knows the garden sorts of *Dianthus* because Perdita includes 'gillyvors' in *The Winter's Tale*:

. . . our carnations and streaked gillyvors,
Which some call nature's bastards. Of that kind
Our rustic garden's barren, and I care not
To get slips of them.
The Winter's Tale, Act 4 scene 4

Perdita and Polixenes argue about the rights and wrongs of 'meddling' with nature. Perdita says she does not want to take slips (a side shoot with a 'heel' pulled from the parent plant) of carnations for her 'rustic' garden, while Polixenes does not see the harm and goes on to applaud the 'art' that marries 'a gentler scion to the wildest stock'. In this discourse, Shakespeare was tapping into a current debate among garden owners, botanists and scientific thinkers, and at the same time demonstrating that he was familiar with the techniques of propagation and grafting.

OPPOSITE Double pinks, carnations and gillyflowers from John Gerard's *Herball* of 1597 indicate the wide range of *Dianthus* that were being grown in Elizabethan gardens.

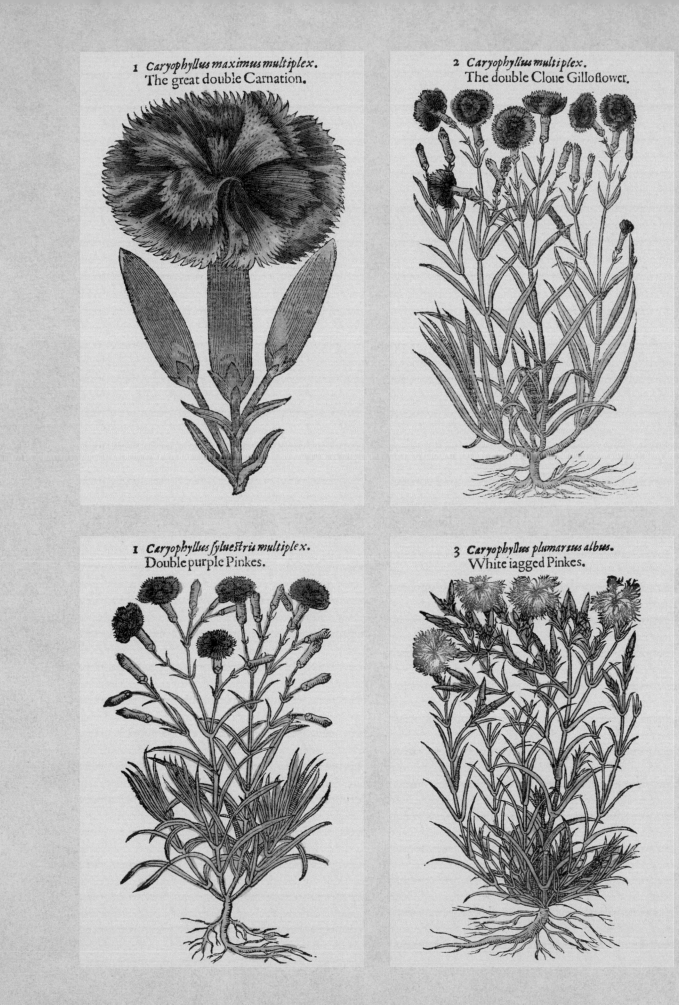

1 *Caryophyllus maximus multiplex.*
The great double Carnation.

2 *Caryophyllus multiplex.*
The double Cloue Gilloflower.

1 *Caryophyllus syluestris multiplex.*
Double purple Pinkes.

3 *Caryophyllus plumarius albus.*
White iagged Pinkes.

Opium poppy (*Papaver somniferum*) (in flower); opium poppy (seed heads); monkshood (*Aconitum napellus*); and wormwood (*Artemisia absinthium*)

Shakespeare touches on the supernatural most notably in *Macbeth*, written against a backdrop of rising religious suspicion, superstition and witch trials in the aftermath of the Gunpowder Plot of 1605 – the plan to murder James I and those in his parliament. The cauldron stirred by the three witches in *Macbeth* probably has the most wild and risky set of ingredients, including 'root of hemlock digged i' th' dark'.[7] Hemlock was listed by Turner as a poison – the remedy for which was to drink hot pure wine.[8] Shakespeare could well have read Turner or Gerard as well as consulted John Hall. Gerard warned that the leaves, seeds and juice of henbane taken inwardly would 'cause an unquiet sleep, like unto the sleep of drunkenness which continueth long, is deadly to the party'.[9] This sounds very much like the drug that Lady Macbeth used to knock out King Duncan's companions long enough for Macbeth to commit the bloody murder of the king.

In real life, women walked a fine line between being knowledgable collectors of useful plants and straying into apothecary or physician territory, which was highly regulated and defended. Then, a woman could be vulnerable to accusations of witchcraft – a situation that was drawn on by Shakespeare in *Macbeth*.

Aconite (*Aconitum*), from both the yellow wolf's bane (*A. lycoctonum* subsp. *vulparia*) and the dark blue monkshood (*A. napellus*), was known to be a deadly poison. Shakespeare was familiar with it when he had King Henry IV say that brotherly love needs to withstand onslaughts as 'strong as aconitum or rash gunpowder'.[10] Gerard is very clear on the grave effects of aconite (which makes the tongue swell and the eyes hang out), but says monkshood was grown in London gardens of the late 1590s.

The opium poppy (*Papaver somniferum*) and mandrake (*Mandragora officinarum*) are interesting plant choices because neither is native to Britain. They occur in *Othello* where the action is set in Venice and Cyprus. Shakespeare refers to them among 'all the drowsy syrups of the world'.[11] Field poppies (*Papaver rhoeas*) were known, of course, but were feared as looking at them was said to bring on blindness or headaches. They are toxic, but do not have the same effects as opium poppy and were not widely used in medical preparations.

Shakespeare was also very interested in the antidotes to poisons. Friar Laurence in *Romeo and Juliet* finally arrives with the antidote for the poison taken by Juliet. The poison was possibly *Atropa belladonna* – what Gerard called 'sleeping nightshade' and advised readers to banish it from their gardens. The balances and checks of nature are something that fascinated Shakespeare and are put into words by Friar Laurence as he goes to collect the necessary herbs for the antidote in his osier basket: 'For naught so vile that on the earth doth live, But to the earth some special good doth give.'[12]

Ophelia's Grief

There's fennel for you, and columbines. There's rue for you, and here's some for me. We may call it herb-grace o' Sundays. O, you must wear your rue with a difference. There's a daisy. I would give you some violets, but they withered all when my father died. They say a made a good end.

Hamlet, Act 4 scene 5

Ophelia, driven mad by the death of her father and the neglect she has suffered by Hamlet, is the centre of a powerful scene in which she hands out a strange mixture of herbs, weeds and flowers to an imaginary audience. It brings together all the sadness of someone who has lost a loved one as well as demonstrating Shakespeare's understanding of ritual religion, grief and the symbolism of plants.

The most striking example is rue (*Ruta graveolens*), which is known as the 'herb of grace', and is a plant certain to have been grown at Hall's Croft. Rue has a bitter taste and a strong aroma, and became associated with repentance, which, if genuine, brings forgiveness or 'grace' from God. In Shakespeare, rue is also used in *Richard II*, when the gardener plants a bank out of pity for the queen:

Here in this place
I'll set a bank of rue, sour herb of grace.
Rue, even for ruth here shortly shall be seen
In the remembrance of a weeping queen
Richard II, Act 3 scene 4

There's rue for you,
Mrs LESSINGHAM in the Character of OPHELIA.

Ophelia depicted in a London production of *Hamlet*, 1772

The herb was probably introduced into Britain by the Romans but little used until it was reintroduced from southern Europe in 1562. Rue was already known as 'strong medicine'. The seeds – drunk in wine – could, according to John Gerard, act as a 'counterpoison' to 'deadly medicines or the poison of wolf's bane [*Aconitum lycoctonum* subsp. *vulparia*], mushrooms or toadstools, the biting of serpents, the stinging of scorpions, bees, hornets and wasps'.

Churches used a range of plants in their rituals, and Shakespeare often mentions flowers in association with funerals and marriages. In the burial scene of Ophelia, the queen scatters flowers on her grave saying: 'Sweets to the sweet', while Laertes hopes that violets will spring from her body. The death of Ophelia was 'doubtful', that is, she died at her own hand, and as such she should have been buried in unconsecrated ground according to the priest, but she is allowed to rest within the churchyard.

Grief along with depression and other mental illnesses were acknowledged by doctors as being disturbances to the melancholic humour. Shakespeare himself may have been drawing on his own experience of losing his son Hamnet when he writes with compassion about Ophelia.

WATERSIDE WEEDS

There is a willow grows aslant a brook
That shows his hoar leaves in the glassy stream.
Therewith fantastic garlands did she make
Of crow-flowers, nettles, daisies, and long purples,
That liberal shepherds give a grosser name,
But our cold maids do dead men's fingers call them.
Hamlet, Act 4 scene 7

Ophelia goes to her watery end wearing a garland of crow flowers, nettles and daisies – the suggestion being that she is wearing a wedding crown of weeds rather than flowers. From the quotation we can pick out 'crow flowers', which are either buttercups or crowfoots from the *Ranunculus* genus and flowers of the waterside and damp meadows.

Among the other plants mentioned, nettles (*Urtica*) were ubiquitous weeds and used in medicine as an antidote for poisons. Long purples could be *Arum maculatum*, the bog arum, which would be happy near to the brook or it might be the early purple orchid (*Orchis mascula*), which has a unpleasant smell, rather like that left behind by tom cats, and might well have sparked rude names.

Red columbine in Gerard's *Herball*

Common crowfoot or crowflower

THE DEVELOPMENT OF THE HOUSE AND GARDEN

At the time it was built, in 1613, Hall's Croft was the one of the larger houses in Stratford-upon-Avon, although still compact when compared with Shakespeare's New Place, just round the corner on Chapel Street. Perhaps, the Halls were tired of living with Susanna's parents and wanted their own space for Hall's consulting room. Their daughter Elizabeth, Shakespeare's granddaughter, was now five years old and it was time to make their own statement in Stratford.

The original house was one-room wide but probably included a separate kitchen building because of the fire risk. A year after it was built, John and Susanna added an extension running along the back. This was probably for the consulting room – a room that would have looked much as it does today, full of books, herbals, stone and china jars, a pestle and mortar, chairs and tables. Above were sleeping rooms for the family and servants.

The house is timber-framed on a stone foundation, with a gabled roof, tiled with handmade clay tiles. We know little of its history between the seventeenth and nineteenth centuries except that, at some time in the eighteenth century, it

The garden behind Hall's Croft was painted in watercolour by Mrs Male in 1850. The spire of Holy Trinity Church is just visible in the distance.

had been given a rendering, covering up the timber framing and disguising its age. When the SBT bought the house in 1949 for £11,000, the first work they did was to remove the render to reveal the oak frame with its lathe-and-plaster panels.

The first reference to Dr John Hall having lived there was in Halliwell-Phillipps's history of New Place in 1864.[13] At that time, it was known as Cambridge House and soon after was renamed Hall's Croft. In 1851, the house is clearly marked on the Board of Works plan, with an enclosed, high-walled garden in a trapezoidal shape. The mulberry tree is marked – which indicates it was of some age by 1851 – and the map also shows the town boundary which runs right through the centre of the garden – one side being a Pleasure Ground, the other being orchard and vegetable plots. A mid-nineteenth-century watercolour also depicts a decorative garden building with an open front and three Gothic bays. In 1868, the house became a school and the orchard area was turned into a playground. It returned to private use in the twentieth century and, sometime between 1914 and 1938, a path was laid out where the vegetable plots had been, with herbaceous beds either side and a sundial at the end – still *in situ* today.

The view today has changed little since the watercolour (opposite) was painted, and the mulberry tree is still in place.

The garden has always remained in two halves: the part nearest the house sitting in Old Stratford; the part furthest away in the New Town. The SBT decided to emphasize this history, and at the same time deal with changes of levels, by putting in a diagonal walkway to mark the boundary and separate the two halves. They also built a raised terrace against the western wall. In 1999, a herb garden was added to reflect more of the plants mentioned in Dr Hall's casebook.

THE GARDEN TODAY

Hall's Croft still retains its ancient boundary layout and trapezoidal shape, surrounded by high, red-brick walls. The 250-year-old mulberry sits on this boundary line and has been shored up over the years with stone, wood and metal, but essentially this is a mid-twentieth-century formal garden, planted when the SBT took possession of the house.

Along the road boundary, tall pollarded limes (*Tilia*) are underplanted with early crocus, followed in spring by scillas, double daisies (*Bellis perennis*), narcissus and hyacinths. Along the opposite boundary, two poplars have been lopped and

OPPOSITE Two clipped box (*Buxus*) mounds stand on the terrace backed by a spring planting of tulips.
BELOW The lime (*Tilia*) trees along the boundary wall are pollarded regularly. In spring, narcissus, hyacinth and scillas are planted at their feet.

sawn in half lengthways – giving them a quirky appearance – yet they still survive. The early twentieth-century path and borders are still in place, set along their length with standard roses underplanted with irises, delphiniums and later flowering herbacous plants. On the western boundary, steps lead up to a raised brick viewing terrace, which looks down over rose beds edged with box (*Buxus*) and a wide open area of lawn.

The mulberry, which could date to the eighteenth century, has been shored up over the years, but its gnarled, almost horizontal trunk gives character to the garden. In spring, it is surrounded by a circular bed of wallflowers (*Erysimum*), forget-me-nots (*Myosotis*), double daisies (*Bellis*) and orange tulips (*Tulipa* 'Prinses Irene'). This same planting scheme is installed for spring in the narrow border beneath the magnolia and wisteria at the front of the house. This colourful combination of bulbs, hardy annuals and short-lived perennials is something the Elizabethans would have practised as a way of building up

OPPOSITE The old mulberry (*Morus nigra*) tree at Hall's Croft marks the boundary between the old town and the 'new' borough of Stratford-upon-Avon. BELOW Fiery *Crocosmia* 'Lucifer' has been planted all along the double herbaceous borders.

HERBS GROWN AT HALL'S CROFT

bay (*Laurus nobilis*)

bladder campion (*Silene vulgaris*)

cotton lavender (*Santolina chamaecyparissus*)

comfrey (*Symphytum*)

curry plant (*Helichrysum italicum*)

fennel, bronze and green (*Foeniculum*)

hyssop (*Hysoppus officinalis*)

lemon balm (*Melissa officinalis*)

marjoram, silver and gold (*Origanum*)

peppermint (*Mentha × piperita*)

spearmint (*Mentha spicata*)

red valerian (*Centranthus ruber*)

rue (*Ruta graveolens*)

sage, green, purple and tricoloured (*Salvia*)

salad burnet (*Sanguisorba minor*)

small-leaved thyme (*Thymus serphyllum* 'Minor')

thyme, golden, lemon and orange (*Thymus*)

valerian (*Valeriana officinalis*)

wall germander (*Teucrium chamaedrys*)

winter savory (*Satureja montana*)

wormwood (*Artemisia absinthium*)

A recent addition to the garden at Hall's Croft
is the herb garden, laid out in four quarters
to represent the four coloured 'humours' that
physicians would treat.

'It is a wise father that knows his own child'

The Merchant of Venice,
Act 2 scene 2

colour, pattern and texture in the garden – elements that were highly prized in the short growing season.

The main new feature of the garden is the herb garden, planted in quarters to represent the four humours. Red is represented by purple sage (*Salvia*), while golden thymes and marjoram (*Origanum*) zing out from the 'yellow' quarter. Black is represented by dark bronze fennel (*Foeniculum*), while aromatic sage and mint (*Mentha*) lift the 'green' quarter.

A DAUGHTER'S LEGACY

Susanna and John Hall were an interesting couple: he, the devoted doctor, churchwarden and level-headed puritan; she, the 'witty' (clever), strong-minded dissenter (Susanna may have kept up the Catholic faith of her grandparents). At Easter 1606, she is listed as being absent from church – a common stand taken by Catholics who would not take Protestant communion on important church festivals – and for which there was a large fine to pay of £20. She is also listed in the Church Court records (known as the Bawdy Court) five years after her marriage, when she is accused of having an affair with Rafe Smith, a hatter, or more specifically of having given him venereal disease. Although a common accusation, it sounds as if it was designed to bring maximum shame on John Hall, who spent his life trying to cure syphilis and other diseases. Susanna brought an action for slander and, because the accuser – a man called Lane – did not turn up at the hearing, the case was closed.

When Shakespeare died in 1616, Susanna inherited his property and she and John returned to live with her mother Anne at New Place. Susanna lived on into her sixties, and it is likely that her only daughter, Elizabeth, wrote the epitaph on the tomb, which can still be seen in the chancel of Holy Trinity Church, next to her husband and father:

Witty above her sex, but that's not all
Wise to salvation was good Mistress Hall.
Something of Shakespeare was in that, but this
Wholly of him with whom she's now in bliss.

Purple globe thistles (*Echinops ritro*) and tall yellow golden rod (*Solidago*) are mainstays of the summer borders, while *Crocosmia* 'Lucifer' adds a splash of red.

A Man of Property
New Place Garden

His life was gentle, and the elements
So mixed in him that nature might stand up
And say to all the world 'This was a man.'

Julius Caesar, Act 5 scene 5

Of all Shakespeare's family homes, New Place is the most intriguing.
It was Shakespeare's own home, the one that he bought at the age of
thirty-three, with his hard-earned money, and the one where he died
aged fifty-two. Frustratingly, the house is no longer there and what
remains are enigmatic earthworks, which have given rise to several
hundred years of excavation and speculation. Yet, the garden is still
there – changed of course – but not built over; a large open space that
offers clues as to Shakespeare's life. Like all the gardens in this book,
it has its own four-hundred-year history.

The site of Shakespeare's house has remained an open garden space since it was pulled down in the mid-eighteenth century.

ABOVE In the eighteenth century, New Place Garden had a high wall around it. To the left is Nash's House, and beyond is the Guild Chapel and Guildhall where Shakespeare went to school.

OPPOSITE The yew (*Taxus*) hedge along the boundary with Chapel Lane has been fashioned into striking topiary over the years.

CLOPTON'S HOUSE

THE ORIGINAL HOUSE on the corner of Chapel Street and Chapel Lane was already ancient and probably dilapidated when Shakespeare bought it in 1597. According to antiquarian and traveller John Leland, it was a 'pretty house of timber and brick', built by Sir Hugh Clopton before 1496. Clopton had already given Stratford its fourteen-arch stone bridge across the River Avon.

It had been known as the Great House and was leased by one of Henry VIII's physicians – Dr Thomas Bentley – for £10 a year. It was the second largest house in Stratford, being outshone only by 'the College', which was a former ecclesiastical collegiate house near Holy Trinity Church.

Nevertheless, when Shakespeare knew it, it was in 'great ryne and decay'. The records suggest that it always had substantial gardens: in 1563, it was described as New Place Gardyn; and, in 1567, as 'one messuage and one garden' – a messuage being a plot of land with house and outbuildings.

The document that records Shakespeare's acquiring the title of New Place is dated 4 May 1597 and says he paid £60 for it. A murder had been committed in the family of the people selling it (the Underhills). This, added to the fact that it was a ruin, suggests he was buying a house that no one else wanted. Nevertheless, it was listed as having ten chimneys, two barns, two gardens and two orchards. Shakespeare was not wealthy at this point. He had recently joined the Lord Chamberlain's Men, and in two years' time they would build the Globe Theatre and he would become a major shareholder, but just then he belonged to a successful group of players with good patronage, and he is likely to have been paid around £6 per play, plus his acting fees.

Buying New Place could also have been an emotional decision. The year before, Shakespeare's only son Hamnet had died, aged eleven. Now he was establishing a presence in Stratford, somewhere for his wife Anne and his two daughters Judith and Susanna – then aged twelve and fourteen – to call home. The corner plot that Shakespeare bought included the house and two parcels of land on Chapel Lane, one of which contained a barn that was still standing in the nineteenth century. It also had an orchard in what is now known as the Great Garden. Archaeology has shown that the house was probably set back from Chapel Street, with a gatehouse and a range of timber buildings running at a right angle to the house, down Chapel Lane. It was, in essence, a smaller version of the grand garden and house layouts typical of the Elizabethan period, with an entrance building, an inner 'court' and kitchen gardens and orchards lying behind the house.

Very little was known about the history of the garden until the campaign in the nineteenth century by antiquarian James Halliwell-Phillipps to rescue the garden for the nation. In his *Historical Account of New Place* he quotes the following statement about the house from Mr John Jordan, who remembered the Shakespeare family: 'Mr William Shakespeare . . . repaired it . . . and laid out a garden in a handsome manner . . . and in or about 1609 planted a Mulberry Tree.'[1] This idea that the Shakespeares had to repair the house before it was habitable is lent weight by the town records of 1598, which detail the couple passing on their spare stone to the corporation to repair Clopton's Bridge – the way travellers from the south still enter Stratford.

On 4 February 1598, Anne and William Shakespeare's barn was listed as having ten quarters of barley malt stored in it. When set against the backdrop of the poor harvests of the late 1590s, this looks as if Shakespeare was

The fourteen-arch bridge built by Sir Hugh Clopton is the way Shakespeare would have crossed the River Avon into Stratford on his return from London. Stones from New Place were used to repair the fabric in 1598.

protecting his family against hardship or, more likely, making money out of trading a desirable commodity. Malting – the soaking and drying of barley to make malt for brewing ale and beer – was one of the main industries of Stratford-upon-Avon and would be much in demand.

WHAT DID NEW PLACE LOOK LIKE?

Arriving at New Place today, visitors try to reconstruct in their mind what Shakespeare's house actually looked like: where his kitchen garden might have been; whether or not he had a knot garden like the one we see today; and how many fruit trees there were in his orchard. Some of these puzzles may never be resolved, but many are being illuminated by twenty-first-century archaeology and a reinterpretation of the illustrations and records that exist. The picture is complicated because there has been more than one house on the site. Shakespeare's house – the Tudor one – was demolished in 1702 and a new one was put up by the Clopton family (who had repurchased the property).

The only clue we have as to what Shakespeare's house looked like is a sketch of 1737 by a local man, George Vertue, who drew it from memory, forty years after he had seen it. The drawing shows a gabled, half-timbered gatehouse, beyond which was a courtyard and a brick house connected by timber ranges. Vertue wrote on the sketch: 'an outward gate there was before the house itself . . . within a little courtyard, grass growing there . . . the outside being only a long gallery and for servants'. It was clearly large, with room enough for servants, guests and perhaps a first-floor gallery as other Elizabethan houses had. It was certainly large enough for Shakespeare's elder daughter, Susanna, who inherited New Place from her father, to welcome Queen Henrietta Maria (Charles I's queen) for three days in 1643.

THE REVEREND'S REVENGE

Shakespeare's house was remodelled to suit the eighteenth-century taste of Sir John Clopton. But even this house had a short life. It was bought by the Reverend Francis Gastrell, in 1753, and he did not like the numerous tourists coming to his door, asking more often than not to be shown: 'Mr Shakespeare's mulberry' in the garden. In 1758, the Gastrells cut down the mulberry – out of spite (see panel, page 164). The townspeople were naturally outraged, because visitors spent money in their inns and shops. A year later, in 1759, after a violent dispute with the Stratford-upon-Avon Corporation, the Gastrells had the house itself demolished. The shocked townspeople hounded him out of town, and the site of New Place has been 'house-less' ever since.

New Place, however, remained a magnet for Shakespeare enthusiasts fuelled by the actor/manager David Garrick, who, in the mid-eighteenth century, did

The Reverend Gastrell was the incumbent of Holy Trinity Church who bought New Place in 1753. He soon tired of the streams of visitors coming to see Shakespeare's last home and retaliated by cutting down the mulberry tree – and eventually demolished the house itself.

much to revive interest in Shakespeare's plays and the playwright himself. At his own Hampton House near the River Thames at Twickenham with its 'Capability' Brown landscape, Garrick had a temple built to house his recently commissioned bust of Shakespeare by Louis-François Roubiliac – as well as other Shakespearian objects. In 1769, Garrick masterminded an enormous, three-day celebration in Stratford-upon-Avon known as the Jubilee.

In 1827, a Shakespearian Theatre was built on part of the Great Garden behind New Place, while the site of the house became the focus for visitors and theatregoers. In 1861, Halliwell-Phillipps campaigned to raise money to buy the land, and he funded his own excavation of the site in 1862–3. He believed that the gardens were monument enough to Shakespeare and resisted the move to put up more statues to the playwright.

Folk memory in the town remembers the garden being surrounded by wooden pales (which would be typically Elizabethan) but later pictures show a high wall, which was lowered in the nineteenth century. The SBT bought the site in 1884 and replaced the wall with cast-iron railings.

By 1895, the wall around New Place Garden had been replaced by iron railings and the site had become, in essence, a Victorian park, open to the people of Stratford-upon-Avon. In 1897, it came under the care of gardener Frank Jackson, who looked after the grounds for fifty years, until 1947.

Shakespeare's Mulberries

Humble as the ripest mulberry
That will not hold the handling
Coriolanus, Act 3 scene 2

Shakespeare mentions the fruit only twice in his plays: in the above extract and in *A Midsummer Night's Dream*,[2] when Titania's attendant fairies feed them to Nick Bottom. As a fruit it was exotic, although black mulberry trees (*Morus nigra*) had been known in London since at least the fourteenth century.

In 1609, James I issued an order to his lord lieutenants to encourage the planting of mulberry trees across the kingdom. He recommended white mulberries (*M. alba*), the leaves of which can be used to support silkworms. If Britain could produce its own silk, it would not need to rely on imported yarn, which was expensive. Two things went wrong with the king's plan: firstly, white mulberries did not enjoy the climate of Britain and rarely did well; and, secondly, most of the cuttings ordered and subsequently planted were those of the black mulberry. As mulberries are very slow to fruit (often taking ten years or more), it was some time before the mistake was recognized.

Nevertheless, in the early seventeenth century, if you had any land at all – and wanted to please the king – then mulberries were the fashionable thing to plant. The king himself had 1.6 hectares/4 acres west of St James Park (now part of Buckingham Palace) planted with mulberries, while at Oatlands, in Surrey, there was a silk worm house built by Inigo Jones. When James I reclaimed Theobalds in Hertfordshire from Robert Cecil in 1607, he instructed his gardener, Jennings, to plant mulberries. At Hatfield House, John Tradescant the Elder planted hundreds of mulberries as well as thousands of grapevines (*Vitis*). Tradescant would later work at Oatlands under the title of 'Keeper of the Gardens, Vines and Silk Worms'.

The excitement about Shakespeare's mulberry tree, which seems to have been a single tree or perhaps originally a small plantation of young trees, did not begin until 1758, when the then owner of the house, Reverend Gastrell, chopped it down. There were riots in the town, and Gastrell and his family were forced to leave in 1759. Such was the interest – and horror – at the destruction that an enterprising carpenter, Thomas Sharpe, made trinkets from the timber – snuff boxes, goblets and caskets – as mementos to be sold to visitors. Many more of these survive than could possibly be genuine, but several date from the mid-eighteenth century and are made from mulberry wood.

So where was the original tree, which would have been around 150 years old when it was cut down by Gastrell? In the Great Garden there are two surviving mulberries. One is an offspring of the older tree, planted by the actress Dame Peggy Ashcroft in 1969, but the other mulberry could well be on the site of the original Shakespeare one – it is itself several hundred years old and has been protected with a stone wall and various supports. Whatever the truth, Shakespeare mulberries have sprung up in many gardens – claiming to be descended from the original. One of the oldest is at Hall's Croft (see page 151) and certainly two-hundred-and-fifty years old. One of the problems with mulberries is that, although slow to establish and fruit, once growing they soon develop the gnarled appearance that suggests great age.

One thing does seem clear, though. The trees planted in Shakespeare's gardens are all black mulberries – and with their sweet, hand-staining fruit these are surely the ones he knew. The fruit of the white mulberry is sharper and less palatable.

TOP This writing standish made by Thomas Sharpe is said to have been carved from 'Shakespeare's mulberry tree'.

ABOVE The oldest mulberry in the Great Garden at New Place was here pictured in 1900.

RIGHT Black mulberry (*Morus nigra*)

THE SHAKESPEARES AT NEW PLACE

Until his death, Shakespeare continued his connections with London and the theatre world. However, even among the scant records of his life, there are clues that New Place became the centre of his property, land and business dealings. He or Anne let out at least part of the house to Thomas Greene and his wife. (Greene was a lawyer practising at the Middle Temple in London, who later became the town clerk of Stratford-upon-Avon.) As the house was big enough for more than one family, the Greene family lived at New Place for many years alongside Anne, Susanna and Judith.

In 1602, Shakespeare bought 43.3 hectares/107 acres of freehold farmland in Old Stratford for the large sum of £320 – most likely for the rents it would bring in. In 1605, he increased his holdings by paying £440 for a half share in the leasehold tithes of various villages around Stratford. By the time of his daughter's marriage to Dr John Hall, he was able to give her a dowry of 40 hectares/100 acres of land. And later, in 1614, he and Dr Hall were asked for their support in disputes about the enclosure of common land in nearby Welcombe, although it is not clear whether he supported the changes or not.

Susanna and her new husband John lived at New Place with the Shakespeares until they built their own house, Hall's Croft, in 1613. Their daughter Elizabeth had been born in 1608, and it is not fanciful to imagine that Shakespeare spent time with the only grandchild he would know in the garden at New Place. During his time as owner of New Place, he wrote more than twenty plays including many of the ones that have strong family themes: *Hamlet, Macbeth* and *King Lear*. His last solo play was *The Tempest* in 1611 – his last three plays having been written in conjunction with John Fletcher. The fire that burnt down the Globe in 1613 may have compounded his decision to spend more time in Stratford-upon-Avon, but he may also have been suffering ill health.

Shakespeare lived to see his younger daughter, Judith, marry Thomas Quiney, the son of his old friend Richard Quiney, but he was unsure enough about the match (Quiney had got another woman pregnant in the run-up to the wedding) to change his will. Shakespeare died at New Place and was buried in Holy Trinity Church, a few hundred metres from his home, on 23 April 1616 – the day on which it is believed that he was born.

NASH'S HOUSE AND THE GREAT GARDEN

Formerly, visitors arriving to see Shakespeare's house were ushered into the house next door. This is known as Nash's House and is a handsome gentleman's residence of the seventeenth century. It would have been physically joined to New Place, sharing a frontage on to Chapel Street, and it was bought sometime after 1637 by Thomas Nash, a prominent Stratford citizen. Elizabeth,

BELOW The final items Shakespeare left were his will and his 'lost' seal ring – found in 1810, near Holy Trinity Church and now one of the treasures held at The Shakespeare Centre in Stratford-upon-Avon.

OPPOSITE This oil portrait by Gerard Soest was painted between 1660 and 1680. It is based on the John Taylor's Chandos portrait, now held in the National Portrait Gallery, which depicts William Shakespeare c.1610, when he would have been forty-five or forty-six years of age.

RIGHT This early seventeenth-century painting has long been associated with Shakespeare's granddaughter Elizabeth and her husband Thomas Nash, who bought the house next door to New Place. The likenesses of the portraits have not been substantiated, but the dress is typical of the early Jacobean period.

OPPOSITE Shakespeare's granddaughter Elizabeth married Thomas Nash, who owned the property adjoining New Place, now called Nash's House.

Shakespeare's granddaughter, who was eight when her grandfather died, was married to Nash for twenty years, and their house, furnished with oak refectory tables, carved cupboards and upholstered chairs, is in the style that the Shakespeares would have had next door at New Place. Elizabeth inherited both houses, although, after Thomas Nash's death, she married John (later Sir John) Barnard and went to live at Abington Manor in Northamptonshire.

The open area of lawn behind New Place and Nash's House has always been known as the Great Garden. It may have been called 'Great' because it went with the 'Great House' – an older name for New Place. Yet, it seems likely that the land from the two properties were joined at some point. Shakespeare's orchard and kitchen garden would probably have been situated here, with the knot garden (if there was one) nearer to the house.

NASH'S
HOUSE
AND
THE SITE OF
NEW PLACE

RIGHT Ernest Law's knot garden of the 1920s was laid out to a pen-and-ink design by Frederick Christian Wellshood. Based on original Elizabethan designs, this plan was used again in the twenty-first century, to refresh the knot garden at New Place.

OPPOSITE ABOVE Law decided to site the new knot garden just behind Nash's House (shown on the right in this picture taken in 1900) and he used almost the full width of the plot.

OPPOSITE BELOW The finished knot garden was opened in 1922 to great acclaim. The standard roses were donated by the royal family, and espaliered fruit trees were planted against the oak trellis. The Great Garden can be glimpsed through the trellis at the top of the picture.

DEVELOPMENT OF NEW PLACE GARDEN

Throughout the Victorian and Edwardian era, New Place Garden remained park-like in its layout with the old foundations of the house grassed over, an old well covered with ivy (*Hedera*), and winding paths among the shrubs and trees. However, after Nash's House underwent restoration from 1910 to 1920, attention turned again to the garden and to the idea that its 'Shakespearian' elements were not being celebrated.

The Tudor historian Ernest Law, who was one of the trustees of the SBT (and would go on to advise and direct the knot garden at Hampton Court), believed that New Place should have a knot garden. In 1922, by raising public subscriptions and patronage from the royal family, he designed and created a sunken parterre/knot, with a wooden arbour tunnel and a 'wildflower bank' – devised by designer Miss Ellen Wilmott who was also working at Anne Hathaway's Cottage (see page 96). It was Law also who disliked the 'ugly' Victorian cast-iron railings and suggested the planting of the yews (*Taxus*) all along Chapel Lane. These have now grown into the characterful topiary shapes that almost obscure the railings. Law also designed the yew buttresses that

OPPOSITE Ellen Willmott's wild bank at New Place was inspired by Shakespeare's references to flowers. The plants depicted here from John Gerard's *Herball* of 1597 are (clockwise, from top left): wild thyme; wild white thyme; upright heartsease; and purple garden violet.

compartmentalize the 90 metre/295 foot border, which has been designed to provide late summer and autumn colour.

The idea of a knot garden sparked the public imagination and donations of plants poured in from gardens with Shakespearian links, including Wilton House, Charlecote, Glamis, Cawdor, Burghley and Cobham Hall. The garden was to be surrounded by a trellis of Warwickshire oak on to which were trained crab apples (*Malus*) and roses. The knot – set out in box (*Buxus*), thrift (*Armeria maritima*), cotton lavender (*Santolina chamaecyparissus*) and thyme – was based on those illustrated in *The Gardeners Labyrinth* by Thomas Hill. The royal family sent four standard roses – one each from King George, Queen Mary, Queen Alexander and the Prince of Wales – and these were placed in the centre of each bed.

Ellen Wilmott's Wild Bank[3] at the back of the garden closely followed the one described in Francis Bacon's essay *Of Gardens* written in 1625, using eglantine roses (*Rosa rubiginosa*), honeysuckle (*Lonicera*), violets, primroses (*Primula vulgaris*) and thyme – to represent Titania's bower:

> I know a bank where the wild thyme blows,
> Where oxlips and the nodding violet grows,
> Quite overcanopied with luscious woodbine,
> With sweet musk-roses, and with eglantine.
> There sleeps Titania sometime of the night,
> Lulled in these flowers with dances and delight;
> *A Midsummer Night's Dream*, Act 2 scene 1

Presumably, Law did not share Bacon's opinion of knots, which is unequivocal: 'As for the making of knots . . . they be but toys; you may see as good sights many times in tarts.'

UNRAVELLING THE GARDEN ARCHAEOLOGY

The question is, was Law's knot garden put in the right place? And what evidence is there that Shakespeare had a knot garden or any other garden features? In making a knot garden, Shakespeare would, of course, have been following many examples that he might have seen at Elizabeth I's palaces, and perhaps at Dudley's Kenilworth Castle, so it is not unthinkable.

The first excavation was by Halliwell-Phillipps in 1862–3, which confirmed the foundations of the range of service buildings along Chapel Lane although not the house itself. Between 2009 and 2013, Birmingham Archaeology carried out extensive work and confirmed that Halliwell's foundations were correct; they also unearthed the limestone rubble 'footings' of timber-framed walls

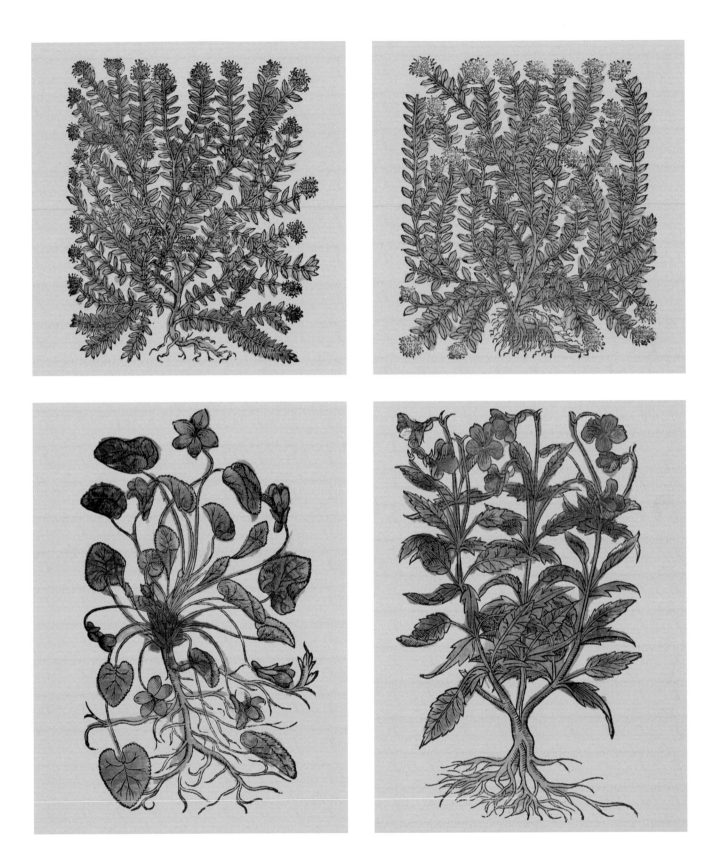

Violets and Pansies

That strain again it had a dying fall.
O, it came o'er my ear like the sweet sound
That breathes upon a bank of violets,
Stealing and giving odour.
Twelfth Night, Act 1 scene 1

Shakespeare mentions violets in connection with their colour, their uses and most often their scent. From the reference to perfume, we must assume he is referring to *Viola odorata* – the native 'sweet' violet that grows wild below shady hedges, banks and on woodland edges. The common dog violet (*V. riviniana*) is equally pretty, but unscented; in Warwickshire, its local name was 'summer violet' and it does flower later – April to June, rather than the more normal months of February to May.

THE UBIQUITOUS VIOLET

Violets were loved equally by rich and poor – as a pretty wild flower to collect from the hedgerow or to transplant into country gardens, or as a smart bedding plant for the knot gardens of the Elizabethan elite. By the late sixteenth century, there are purple, white and double varieties of the simple violet being grown in gardens. They were used to perfume oil, as strewing flowers at the graveside, and as an ingredient of garlands, nosegays and posies

Shakespeare features violets in his first published work, *Venus and Adonis*:

These blue-veined violets whereon we lean
Never can blab, nor know not what we mean.
Venus and Adonis, lines 125–6

When Shakespeare wrote 'When daisies pied and violets blue'[4] he may have been referring to the common dog violet, which prefers a more open aspect than the scented violet, and would have made a good choice to sit among daisies (*Bellis*) and lady's smock (*Cardamine*

pratensis). However, in *Henry V* and *Hamlet*, it is clearly the scented violet that is the subject matter:

I think the king is but a man, as I am. The violet smells to him as it doth to me; the element shows to him as it doth to me.
Henry V, Act 4 scene 1

A violet in the youth of primy nature,
Forward not permanent, sweet not lasting,
The perfume and suppliance of a minute,
Hamlet, Act 1 scene 3

LOVE-IN-IDLENESS

There is another well-known viola referred to by Shakespeare – the tricoloured heartsease pansy (*Viola tricolor*). When Ophelia says of pansies, 'that's for thoughts', she is referring to the French word for thoughts, '*pensées*'. However, *Viola tricolor* (from which our modern pansies are bred) was also known for soothing the heart, hence its common name heartsease. In *A Midsummer Night's Dream*, Shakespeare is probably playing on its common names, 'heartsease' and 'love-in-idleness', when Oberon claims that the juice of it will make Titania fall madly in love with the first creature she sees on waking.[5]

Gerard features two types in his *Herball*: the ordinary heartsease and the upright heartsease. Violas and pansies were widely used as an 'infill' plant for knot gardens, along with marigolds, pinks and daisies.

Heartsease (*Viola tricolor*)

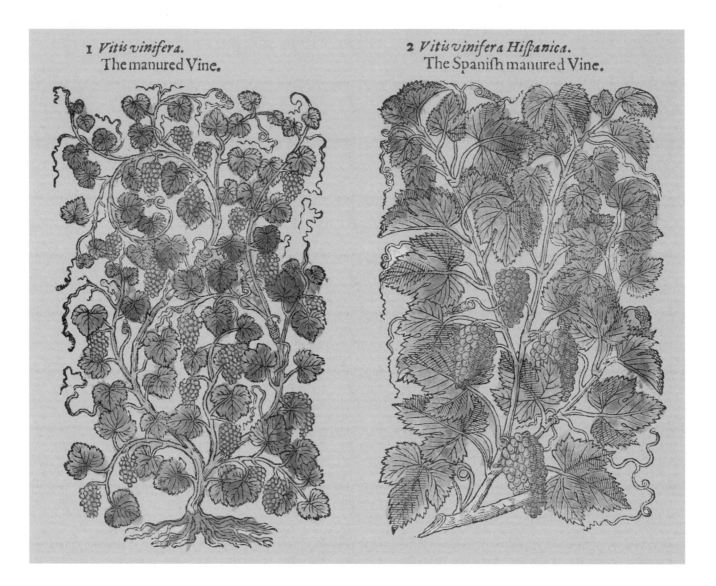

1 *Vitis vinifera.*
The manured Vine.

2 *Vitis vinifera Hiſpanica.*
The Spaniſh manured Vine.

Grapevines (*Vitis*) as garden plants were becoming popular among those with the space and time to cultivate them. There are records of vines being grown at New Place in the early seventeenth century.

in the central area of the site. The south-east quadrant of the knot garden revealed the foundations of some Tudor brick outbuildings and rubbish pits, so it looks likely that Law built his 1920s knot garden over an unidentifiable outside space. In 2015, a rare chance to do archaeology at the front of the property confirmed the positions of at least two of the walls of the inner house as well as evidence of Tudor ovens and cold storage pits, which would have belonged to the Shakespeares' house. But as to the garden, the archaeology is silent – which is to be expected if, as stated in the first chapter, Elizabethan gardens were mainly ephemeral.

Nevertheless, the few finds and documents shed just a glimmer of light on William and Anne's house and the suggestion that they 'laid out

a garden in a handsome manner'. There is a letter indicating that the garden had vines, if not a small vineyard. In an inventory of the house and contents in 1753, the year Reverend Gastrell bought New Place, there is mention of a wilderness (perhaps an area of shrubs and paths laid out for walks) and a sundial. Such hints are intriguing.

It is not at all unthinkable that Shakespeare, in the last twenty years of his life, should be interested in creating a garden to reflect his hard-won status. With a coat of arms and a growing reputation, why should he not try and design something to rival the grand Elizabethan houses of other counties. Perhaps too he might have wished to copy some of the fashionable garden 'devices' of the day: the sundials, the knots and the mulberry trees.

A new landscape garden has replaced the open space at the front of New Place Garden, the site of Shakespeare's house.

BELOW This totally new landscape design protects the archaeology while guiding visitors through a twenty-first century space to the historic knot garden and borders beyond.

OPPOSITE The Ernest Law 1920s knot garden, pictured, has been replanted with interwoven ribbons of thyme, box, lavender and santolina infilled with oregano, hyssop and chamomile.

THE GARDEN TODAY

The year 2016 marked a new phase in the story of New Place. With archaeology completed as far as possible at this current time, the soil has been replaced to protect the foundations of Shakespeare's house and a new garden design has been put in place in this Grade II listed park and garden.

A wooden slatted entrance with a bronze surround hints at the gatehouse that Shakespeare had, but is not a pastiche of it. Within the site, the footprint of the courtyard, service buildings and inner house has been reflected in the zoning of the garden – a conceptual interpretation of its four-hundred-year

history. This is an unashamedly twenty-first-century garden using the best landscaping materials, which will increase the garden's accessibility.[6]

Ernest Law's 1920s knot garden has been given a completely new planting plan following the original design and the paths have been made wider and the oak arbour has more 'viewing' openings on to the knot garden. The original espalier fruit trees around the walls are approaching one hundred years old, and may well last another century.

In the Great Garden, Law's yew-buttressed borders remain and the planting reflects his aim to make them look good from summer onwards. The old mulberries have been carefully managed, lifting the crown of the oldest one and installing oak-clad permanent 'props' under the younger one, which was in danger of splitting. Already, there are signs of regeneration – mulberries are happiest as multi-stemmed specimens and these should go on creating interesting shapes for years to come.

BELOW LEFT AND BELOW RIGHT These contemporary, Shakespeare-inspired sculptures are by Greg Wyatt. OPPOSITE In the new scheme, the old infill of colourful bedding plants, pictured, has been replaced with *Thymus serpyllum* 'Raspberry Ripple' and *Origanum vulgare* 'Thumble's Variety'.

'Our little life
Is rounded with
a sleep'

The Tempest, Act 4 scene 1

SHIFTING TIME

As Shakespeare reached maturity, the rhythm of the seasonal year was changing. The old calendar had been full of holy days and festivities, many of which were now a distant memory. In October 1582 – a month before he married Anne Hathaway – it had been decreed that ten days would be lost from the old Julian calendar, and the Gregorian calendar, which we still follow today, began. This theme of the natural order of things being disrupted occurs repeatedly in Shakespeare's plays – and is perhaps what makes them so resonant. He was a man who had one foot in the past but another very firmly in the present.

Ernest Law perhaps puts into words best why all Shakespeare's properties, but particularly New Place, have continued to fascinate historians and archaeologists to dig deeper into its past: 'Why go grubbing among the old foundations and broken walls of a long since destroyed house and garden', he says, 'except that, by . . . calling up the past we may be helped in the present . . . which holds for us the treasures the poet has bequeathed to all mankind?'[7]

ABOVE Shakespeare is buried in the chancel of Holy Trinity, Stratford-upon-Avon.
OPPOSITE The first Shakespearian Theatre was built in the garden of New Place but was later replaced by one on the riverside, now the Royal Shakespeare Theatre, which can be seen from the garden.

Endnotes

INTRODUCTION

1   The Shakespeare Birthplace Trust was founded in 1847 to save Shakespeare's birthplace for the nation. It went on to acquire all his family homes.
2   The Hosking Houses Trust; www.hoskinghouses.co.uk/.
3   Christopher Thacker (1994), *The Genius of Gardening: The History of Gardens in Britain and Ireland*. London: Weidenfeld & Nicolson, page 54.
4   *Love's Labour's Lost*, Act 1 scene 1, line 241.
5   *Henry IV Part II*, Act 5 scene 3.
6   Reprinted in Esther Singleton (1922), *The Shakespeare Garden*. London: Methuen, pages 327–30.
7   Mark Broch and Paul Edmondson (2009), *Shakespeare Found: A Life Portrait Shakespeare Birthplace Trust*. Norwich: Jarrold, in association with Heritage House Media. See also Stanley Wells (ed.) with Mark Broch, Paul Edmondson, Rupert Featherstone, Anthony Holden, Alastair Laing and Diana Scarisbrick (2009), *Shakespeare Found! A Life Portrait at Last*. Stratford-upon-Avon: Cobbe Foundation and SBT.

SHAKESPEARE'S WORLD

1   *Henry VI Part I*, Act 2 scene 4.
2   Thacker (1994), page 54.
3   *A Midsummer Night's Dream*, Act 2 scene 1, lines 251–2.
4   Roy C. Strong (1979), *The Renaissance Garden in England*. London: Thames & Hudson, page 42.
5   Strong (1979), page 45.
6   Thomasina Beck (1997), *Gardening with Silk and Gold: A History of Gardens in Embroidery*. Newton Abbot: David & Charles, page 37.
7   Charles Estienne, Jean Liébault and Richard Surflet (1600), *Maison Rustique or The Countrie Farm*. Compiled in the French tongue by Charles Steuens and Iohn Liebault doctors of physicke. And translated into English by Richard Surflet practitioner in physicke. Printed London: by Adam Islip for John Bill, 1616, page 339 and others.
8   Markham quoted in Strong (1979), page 40.
9   26 December.
10 Michael Wood (2003), *In Search of Shakespeare*; 2005 edn: London: BBC Books, page 309.
11 http://www.richmond.gov.uk/local_history_notes/.
12 Wood (2003), page 277.
13 Thomas Platter reported in Strong (1979), page 39.
14 Anna Keay and John Watkins (eds) (2013), *The Elizabethan Garden at Kenilworth Castle*. Swindon: English Heritage.
15 Richard K. Morris (2010), *Kenilworth Castle*. London: English Heritage, page 31.

THE STRATFORD BOY

1   Nicholas A.D. Molyneux (2014c), 'A conservation plan for Shakespeare's birthplace garden, Henley Street, Stratford-upon-Avon'. Commissioned by the SBT from English Heritage, page 5.
2   I am grateful to a lecture given by Roger Pringle, former director of the SBT for providing the chronological outline of the garden at Henley Street as well as Molyneux (2014c). Roger Pringle (2014), 'Shakespeare's Gardens', lecture 23 September.
3   *Hamlet*, Act 4 scene 5, line 175.
4   Letter quoted in Appendix to Molyneux (2014c), SBT TR46/1/116.
5   *Macbeth*, Act 1 scene 1 and Act 1 scene 3.

A COUNTRY CHILDHOOD

1   Brian K. Roberts (1965), 'Settlement, land use and population in the Forest of Arden, Warwickshire, 1086–1350: a study in historical geography'. Unpublished thesis held at SBT archive, page 85.
2   Roberts (1965), page 90.
3   Lucy Toulmin Smith (ed.) (1906), *The Itinerary of John Leland*, Vol. X. London: Bell.
4   V.H.T. Skipp (1970), 'Economic and social change in the Forest of Arden 1530–1649', *Agricultural History Review*, Vol. 18, pages 89–90.
5   Twigs Way (2006), *Virgin Weeders and Queens: A History of Women in the Garden*. Stroud: Sutton, page 8.
6   Way (2006), page vi.
7   N.W. Alcock and R. Bearman (2000), 'Discovering Mary Arden's House', *Shakespeare Quarterly*, Vol. 53, pages 53–82.
8   *The Winter's Tale*, Act 4 scene 3, line 5.
9   James Walter (1890), *Shakespeare's True Life. Illustrated by Gerald E. Moira*. London: James Walter, page 69.
10 Using the calculation of 1 yardland = 12 hectares/30 acres; Nicholas A.D. Molyneux (2014d), 'A conservation plan for Mary Arden's farm garden, Wilmcote, Warwickshire'. Commissioned by the SBT from English Heritage.
11 *Henry IV Part I*, Act 2 scene 5, lines 57–8.
12 Joan Thirsk, in Mary Anne Caton (ed.) (1999), *Fooles and Fricassees: Food in Shakespeare's England*. Washington, DC: Folger Shakespeare Library, University of Washington Press, especially essay by Joan Thirsk, 'Food in Shakespeare's England', page 16.

13   William Turner (1538/1548), *Libellus de re Herbaria* (1538) and *The Names of Herbes* (1548); 1965 edn: introduction by James Britten, B. Daydon Jackson and W.T. Stearn. London: Ray Society, page 74.

14   *The Merry Wives of Windsor*, Act 5 scene 5, line 18.

15   *As You Like It*, Act 5, all of scene 1.

YOUTH AND ROMANCE

1   For a history of the garden's development I am indebted to two sources: Nicholas A.D. Molyneux (2014a), 'A conservation plan for Anne Hathaway's Cottage, Shottery', commissioned by the SBT from English Heritage. Also Roger Pringle (2014).

2   Mary Russell Mitford (1893). *Our Village*. London and New York: Macmillan.

3   *The Tempest*, Act 5 scene 1, line 89.

4   SBT Minutes 1914–1937 TN2/1/3, page 214.

5   On the links between Shakespeare and Drayton, see Roger Pringle (2013), 'The muses quiet port: Clifford Chambers and Michael Drayton', in *Around the Square and Up the Tower*. Stratford-upon-Avon: Hosking Houses Trust, pages 38–47.

6   *The Two Noble Kinsmen*, Act 1 scene 1, line 5.

7   A scheme run by the UK government to encourage sustainable and environmental good practice in farming and managed by Natural England; www.gov.uk/environmental stewardship/.

8   Harvest Share is a community fruit collection and distribution scheme; www.transitionstratford.com/.

9   *Much Ado About Nothing*, Act 2 scene 3, line 3.

10   *As You Like It*, Act 3 scene 2, line 118.

11   *The Taming of the Shrew*, Act 2 scene 1, line 228.

THE GARDEN VISITOR

1   The Shakespeare versus Lambert Case 1588–9. Jonathan Bate (2009), *Soul of the Age: The Life, Mind and World of William Shakespeare*. London: Penguin, pages 322–3 gives an early date for Shakespeare being in London to instruct attorney Harborne in late summer 1588 at St Clements Danes or in his chambers at Middle Temple.

2   *Henry VI Part I*, Act 2, all of scene 4.

3   *Henry IV Part II*, Act 3 scene 2, lines 12–15.

4   *The Merry Wives of Windsor*, Act 3 scene 3, line 67.

5   His younger brother Edmund, who followed him to London in the late 1590s as a seventeen-year-old boy, may have lodged with him. On Edmund see: Bate (2009), pages 48–9.

IN SICKNESS AND IN HEALTH

1   There are no documents to prove who owned Hall's Croft before 1627. Other possible candidates for where the Halls could have lived include the Dower House and St Mary's, see Nicholas A.D. Molyneux (2014b), 'A conservation plan for Hall's Croft Garden, Old Town, Stratford-upon-Avon'. Commissioned by the SBT from English Heritage, page 21.

2   *Pericles, Prince of Tyre*, all of scene 12.

3   *Cymbeline*, Act 5 scene 6, lines 249–58.

4   Joan Lane (1996), *John Hall and His Patients: The Medical Practice of Shakespeare's Son-in-Law*. Stratford-upon-Avon: SBT.

5   *The Winter's Tale*, Act 4 scene 3, line 44.

6   *Romeo and Juliet*, Act 2 scene 2; see also Act 4 scene 1.

7   *Macbeth*, Act 4 scene 1, line 25.

8   William Turner (1551), *A New Herball*; 1989 edn: Chapman, George T.L. and Tweddle, Marilyn N. (eds). Manchester: Carcanet Press, in association with Mid-Northumberland Arts Group, page 141.

9   John Gerard (1597a), *The General Historie of Plants*; 1927 edn: Woodward, Marcus (ed.); 1994 edn: London: Studio Editions, page 87.

10   *Henry IV Part II*, Act 4 scene 3, line 48.

11   *Othello*, Act 3 scene 3, line 335.

12   *Romeo and Juliet*, Act 2 scene 2, lines 17–18.

13   J.O. Halliwell-Phillipps (1864), *An Historical Account of New Place, Stratford-upon-Avon, The Last Residence of Shakespeare*. London: Printed by J.E. Adlar.

A MAN OF PROPERTY

1   Halliwell-Phillipps (1864), page 19.

2   *A Midsummer Night's Dream*, Act 3 scene 1, line 159.

3   Ernest Law (1922), *Shakespeare's Garden*. Stratford-upon-Avon: Selwyn & Blount, page 23.

4   *Love's Labour's Lost*, Act 5 scene 2, line 879.

5   *A Midsummer Night's Dream*, Act 2 scene 1, lines 165–72.

6   The design for New Place Garden is by Expedition (architects: Chris Wise and Tim O'Brien). Landscaping is by Gillespies Landscape Architects. The project involved a team of artists, makers and structural engineers as well as the SBT gardeners under Scott Boyden. It is managed by the SBT New Place Project team. Archaeology has been carried out by teams from Birmingham and Staffordshire universities.

7   Law (1922), page 34.

Bibliography

(Original edition is cited first; any later editions used as reference appear at the end of the appropriate entry)

GENERAL
Wells, Stanley, Taylor, Gary, Jowett, John and Montgomery, William (eds) (2005), *The Oxford Shakespeare: The Complete Works*. Oxford: Clarendon Press

BOOKS ABOUT SHAKESPEARE'S LIFE AND WORK
Bate, Jonathan (1998), *The Genius of Shakespeare*; 2008 edn: London: Picador

Bate, Jonathan (2009), *Soul of the Age: The Life, Mind and World of William Shakespeare*. London: Penguin

Broch, Mark and Edmondson, Paul (2009), *Shakespeare Found: A Life Portrait Shakespeare Birthplace Trust*. Norwich: Jarrold, in association with Heritage House Media

Donnelly, Ann and Woledge, Elizabeth (2010), *Shakespeare: Work, Life and Times: Official Guide*. Stratford-upon-Avon: Shakespeare Birthplace Trust; 2012 edn: Norwich: Jigsaw in association with the SBT

Greer, Germaine (2007), *Shakespeare's Wife*. London: Bloomsbury

Nicholl, Charles (2007), *The Lodger: Shakespeare on Silver Street*, London: Allen Lane; 2008 edn: London: Penguin

Shakespeare : work, life and times : official guide / [by Ann and Elizabeth].

Shapiro, James (2005), *1599: A Year in the Life of William Shakespeare*. London: Faber & Faber

Walter, James (1890), *Shakespeare's True Life*. Illustrated by Gerald E. Moira. London: James Walter

Wells, Stanley (1981), *Shakespeare: An Illustrated Dictionary*; 1985 edn: Oxford: Oxford University Press

Wells, Stanley (ed.) with Broch, Mark, Edmondson, Paul, Featherstone, Rupert, Holden, Anthony, Laing, Alastair and Scarisbrick, Diana (2009), *Shakespeare Found! A Life Portrait at Last*. Stratford-upon-Avon: Cobbe Foundation and SBT

Wood, Michael (2003), *In Search of Shakespeare*; 2005 edn: London: BBC Books

BOOKS ABOUT PLANTS AND GARDEN HISTORY
Beck, Thomasina (1997), *Gardening with Silk and Gold: A History of Gardens in Embroidery*. Newton Abbot: David & Charles

Blamey, Marjorie and Grey-Wilson, Christopher (1989), *The Illustrated Flora of Britain and Northern Europe*. London: Hodder & Stoughton

Campbell-Culver, Maggie (2001), *The Origin of Plants*; 2004 edn: London: Eden Project Books

Ellacombe, Henry Nicholson (1884), *The Plant-Lore and Garden-Craft of Shakespeare*. London: Satchell

Fearnley-Whittingstall, Jane (2002), *The Garden: An English Love Affair*. London: Weidenfeld & Nicolson

Fox, Levi (1977), *Shakespeare's Flowers*. Norwich: Jarrold, in association with the SBT

Griffiths, Mark (2015), *Country Life*, Vol. ccix, No. 21 (20 May), pages 120–38

Grigson, Geoffrey (1955), *The Englishman's Flora*. London: Dent; 1987 edn: foreword by Jane Grigson and introduction by W.T. Stearn

Hobhouse, Penelope (1992), *Plants in Garden History*. London: Pavilion

Keay, Anna and Watkins, John (eds) (2013), *The Elizabethan Garden at Kenilworth Castle*. Swindon: English Heritage

Law, Ernest (1922), *Shakespeare's Garden*. Stratford-upon-Avon: Selwyn & Blount

Mitford, Mary Russell (1893). *Our Village*. London and New York: Macmillan

Morgan, Joan and Richards, Alison (1993), *The Book of Apples*. London: Ebury Press, in association with the Brogdale Horticultural Trust

Morris, Richard K. (2010), *Kenilworth Castle*. London: English Heritage

Pringle, Roger (2014), 'Shakespeare Gardens'; lecture given by this former director of the SBT at the Shakespeare Centre, Stratford-upon-Avon, 23 September

Scott-James, Anne (1982), *The Cottage Garden*. London: Penguin

Sinclair-Rohde, Eleanor (1972), *The Old English Gardening Books*. London: Minerva Press

Singleton, Esther (1922), *The Shakespeare Garden*. London: Methuen

Strong, Roy C. (1979), *The Renaissance Garden in England*. London: Thames & Hudson

Strong, Roy C. (2000), *The Artist & The Garden*. New Haven, CT and London: Yale University Press, in association with Paul Mellon Centre for Studies in British Art

Thacker, Christopher (1994), *The Genius of Gardening: The History of Gardens in Britain and Ireland*. London: Weidenfeld & Nicolson

Thomas, Vivian and Faircloth, Nicki (2013), *Shakespeare's Plants and Gardens: A Dictionary*. London: Bloomsbury Academic

Toulmin Smith, Lucy (ed.) (1906), *The Itinerary of John Leland*, Vol. X. London: Bell.

Vickery, Roy (1995), *A Dictionary of Plant Lore*. Oxford: Oxford University Press

Way, Twigs (2006), *Virgin Weeders and Queens: A History of Women in the Garden*. Stroud: Sutton

Way, Twigs (2013), *The Tudor Garden*. Oxford: Shire Publications

REPRINTS OF ORIGINAL TEXTS

Gerard, John (1597a), *The General Historie of Plants*; 1927 edn: Woodward, Marcus (ed.); 1994 edn: London: Studio Editions

Lane, Joan (1996), *John Hall and His Patients: The Medical Practice of Shakespeare's Son-in-Law*. Stratford-upon-Avon: SBT

Turner, William (1538/1548), *Libellus de re Herbaria* (1538) and *The Names of Herbes* (1548); 1965 edn: introduction by James Britten, B. Daydon Jackson and W.T. Stearn. London: Ray Society

Turner, William (1551), *A New Herball*; 1989 edn: Chapman, George T.L. and Tweddle, Marily N. (eds). Manchester: Carcanet Press, in association with Mid-Northumberland Arts Group

Tusser, Thomas (1573), *Five Hundred Points of Good Husbandry*; 1984 edn: introduction by Geoffrey Grigson. Oxford: Oxford University Press

ORIGINAL TEXTS (HELD BY SBT ARCHIVE)

Estienne, Charles, Liébault, Jean and Surflet, Richard (1600), *Maison Rustique or The Countrie Farm. Compiled in the French tongue by Charles Steuens and Iohn Liébault doctors of physicke. And translated into English by Richard Surflet practitioner in physicke*. Printed London: by Adam Islip for John Bill, 1616

Gerard, John (1596), 'Catalogus arborum, fruticum ac plantarum tam indigenarum, quam exoticarum', in *Horto Johannis Gerardi Ciuis & Chirurgic*. Londinensis nascentium Londini: Ex officina Arnoldi Hatfield, impensis Johannis Norton, 1599

Gerard, John (1597b), *The Herball or Generall Historie of Plantes Gathered by Iohn Gerarde of London Master in Chirurgerie*. Engraver William Rogers. Imprinted at London by Edmund Bollifant for Bonham and John Norton

Hall, John (1657), *Select Observations on English Bodies: or, Cures Both Empericall and Historical, Performed upon Very Eminent Persons in Desperate Diseases. First written in Latin. Now put into English by James Cooke, practitioner*. London printed for John Sherley at the Golden Pelican in Little Britain

Hill, Thomas (1577), *The Gardeners Labyrinth*. Henry Dethick (ed.), Printed at London by Henry Ballard and E. Allde, 1608

Parkinson, John (1629), *Paradisi in Sole Paradises Terrestris*. John Parkinson (apothecary of London) and A. Switzer (wood-engraver). Printed by Humfrey Lownes and Robert Young at the signe of the Starre on Bread-street hill

OTHER WORKS CONSULTED

Alcock, N.W. and Bearman, R. (2000), 'Discovering Mary Arden's House', *Shakespeare Quarterly*, Vol. 53, pages 53–82

Bearman, R. (ed.) (1997), *The History of an English Borough: Stratford-upon-Avon 1196–1996*. Stroud: Sutton, in association with the SBT

Caton, Mary Anne (ed.) (1999), *Fooles and Fricassees: Food in Shakespeare's England*. Washington, DC: Folger Shakespeare Library, University of Washington Press, especially essay by Joan Thirsk, 'Food in Shakespeare's England', pages 13–25.

Halliwell-Phillipps, J.O. (1864), *An Historical Account of New Place, Stratford-upon-Avon, The Last Residence of Shakespeare*. London: Printed by J.E. Adlard

Pringle, Roger (2013), 'The muses quiet port: Clifford Chambers and Michael Drayton', in *Around the Square and Up the Tower*. Stratford-upon-Avon: Hosking Houses Trust

Skipp, V.H.T. (1970), 'Economic and social change in the Forest of Arden 1530–1649', *Agricultural History Review*, Vol. 18, pages 84–111

UNPUBLISHED LITERATURE

Molyneux, Nicholas A.D. (2014a), 'A conservation plan for Anne Hathaway's Cottage, Shottery'. Commissioned by the SBT from English Heritage

Molyneux, Nicholas A.D. (2014b), 'A conservation plan for Hall's Croft Garden, Old Town, Stratford-upon-Avon'. Commissioned by the SBT from English Heritage

Molyneux, Nicholas A.D. (2014c), 'A conservation plan for Shakespeare's birthplace garden, Henley Street, Stratford-upon-Avon'. Commissioned by the SBT from English Heritage

Molyneux, Nicholas A.D. (2014d), 'A conservation plan for Mary Arden's farm garden, Wilmcote, Warwickshire'. Commissioned by the SBT from English Heritage

Molyneux, Nicholas A.D. (2014e), 'A conservation plan for New Place Gardens, Chapel Street, Stratford-upon-Avon'. Commissioned by the SBT from English Heritage

Roberts, Brian K. (1965), 'Settlement, land use and population in the Forest of Arden, Warwickshire, 1086–1350: a study in historical geography'. Unpublished thesis held at SBT archive

Chronology of Shakespeare's works

Note: Dates given are those accepted and used by scholars of the SBT.

Composition date	Play title
1590–91	*The Two Gentlemen of Verona*
1590–91	*The Taming of the Shrew*
1591	*Henry VI Part II*
1591	*Henry VI Part III*
1592	*Henry VI Part I* (possibly with Thomas Nashe)
1592	*Titus Andronicus* (possibly with George Peele)
1592–3	*Richard III*
1594	*The Comedy of Errors*
1594–5	*Love's Labour's Lost*
1596	*Edward III* (uncertain authorship) printed in 1596
1595	*Richard II*
1595	*Romeo and Juliet*
1595	*A Midsummer Night's Dream*
1596	*King John*
1596–7	*The Merchant of Venice*
1596–7	*Henry IV Part I*
1597–8	*The Merry Wives of Windsor*
1597–8	*Henry IV Part II*
1598	*Much Ado About Nothing*
1598–9	*Henry V*
1599	*Julius Caesar*
1599–1600	*As You Like It*
1600–1601	*Hamlet*
1600–1601	*Twelfth Night or What You Will*
1602	*Troilus and Cressida*
1603	*Measure for Measure*
1603–1604	*Sir Thomas More*
1603–1604	*Othello*
1604–1605	*All's Well That Ends Well*
1605	*Timon of Athens* (with Thomas Middleton)
1605–1606	*King Lear*
1606	*Macbeth* (revised by Thomas Middleton)
1606	*Antony and Cleopatra*
1607	*Pericles* (with George Wilkins)
1608	*Coriolanus*
1609	*The Winter's Tale*
1610	*Cymbeline*
1611	*The Tempest*
1613	*Henry VIII* (*All is True*) (with John Fletcher)
1613	*Cardenio* (with Fletcher; lost)
1613–14	*The Two Noble Kinsmen* (with Fletcher)

Poems

1582–1602	*Sonnets* (published 1609)
1592–3	*Venus and Adonis*
1593–4	*The Rape of Lucrece*
1601	*The Phoenix and the Turtle*
1603–4	*A Lover's Complaint*

Visiting details

The five Shakespeare family homes are cared for by the Shakespeare Birthplace Trust; www.shakespeare.org.uk; tel. +44(0)1789 204016.

Shakespeare's Birthplace
Henley Street, Stratford-upon-Avon, CV37 6QW

Hall's Croft
Old Town, Stratford-upon-Avon, CV37 6BG

New Place Garden
Chapel Street, Stratford-upon-Avon, CV37 6EP

Mary Arden's Farm
Station Road, Wilmcote, Stratford-upon-Avon, CV37 9UN

Anne Hathaway's Cottage
22 Cottage Lane, Shottery, Stratford-upon-Avon, CV37 9HH

OTHER GARDENS
Hampton Court
www.hrp.org.uk/HamptonCourtPalace

Hatfield House
www.hatfield-house.co.uk

Kenilworth Castle
www.english-heritage.org.uk/visit/places/kenilworth-castle

Little Moreton Hall
www.nationaltrust.org.uk/little-moreton-hall

Penshurst Place
www.penshurstplace.com

Titchfield Abbey
www.english-heritage.org.uk/visit/places/titchfield-abbey

The Inns of Court
www.innertemple.org.uk
www.middletemple.org.uk
www.graysinn.org.uk
www.lincolnsinn.org.uk

Index

Acknowledgments

This book has been written with the cooperation and support of the Shakespeare Birthplace Trust. I would particularly like to thank Lynn Beddoe for being enthusiastic about the initial idea of a book on the gardens, as well as Adam Sherratt, Paul Edmondson, Emma Mulveagh and Nic Fulcher, who guided me throughout the process. In addition, I would like to express my gratitude to all the staff of the museum, archive and library, especially Rosalyn Sklar, Andrew Thomas, Helen Hargest, Jennifer Reid and Madeleine Cox. A further thank you to Sharon Lippett, leader of the period interpretation team at Mary Arden's Farm, who helped with the food aspect of the text, and to Scott Boyden, gardens manager, and his team (especially Christopher Cunningham, Mark Gibbs, Steve Knight, David Lawley, Alan Parnham, Jane Shaw and Annamaria Vass) who showed me around and helped with the plant identification.

I am very lucky to have had photographer Andrew Lawson on the project to bring the gardens alive. Thanks are also due to Caroline Foley, editor of *Topiarius*, for advice on the use of box (*Buxus*). At Frances Lincoln Publishers my special thanks go to Andrew Dunn, Helen Griffin and Laura Nicolson. A big thank you to designer Anne Wilson, editor Joanna Chisholm, proofreader Claire Masset, indexer Michèle Clarke and to my agent James Wills at Watson Little.

Finally, this book would not have been completed without the writers' residency offered to me by the Hosking Houses Trust, near Stratford-upon-Avon. Inspired by Virginia Woolf's *A Room of One's Own*, this small trust offers writers' residencies to women over forty with a publishing contract who need a quiet place to work away from other commitments. To find out more go to www.hoskinghouses.co.uk.